My Brief Career

My Brief

The trials of a
young lawyer

Career

Harry Mount

✳ SHORT BOOKS

First published in 2004 by
Short Books
15 Highbury Terrace
London N5 1UP

10 9 8 7 6 5 4 3 2 1

A CIP catalogue record for this book
is available from the British Library.

ISBN 1-904095-69-0

Printed in Great Britain by
Mackays of Chatham Ltd, Kent.

Characters referred to in *My Brief Career*
are composite characters and essentially the author's
inventions, although everything that
takes place is based on real incidents.

To my parents

The following passage is taken from my diary. I wrote it at the end of a long day at a desk in a barristers' chambers in Inner Temple that specialised in libel. I was in the second six months of a year-long pupillage, the apprenticeship that barristers go through after their academic training.

August 2nd

I am writing this at work on my computer, even though I'll have to print it out on a thin piece of paper and paste it into my diary. I would rather do anything than actually look at what I have to do for work.

Here is the last work-related sentence I wrote –

"The court must ask: What testamentary provision would a reasonable man in the position of this deceased have made for the plaintiff in all the circumstances, including the matters set out in s.3?"

I'm afraid that however much I've tried – and God how I've tried in the past ten months – I cannot work up any enthusiasm for writing this sentence, re-reading this sentence or admiring the people who write these sentences. Some of these people are highly intelligent and – more importantly – can stay alert while looking at sentences like this. I cannot stay alert. I do try hard, and look, concentrating intently, at the books and documents, and can usually get the point of any individual sentence. But as far as getting an overview is concerned, of connecting all these individual thoughts, I am lost.

Things are pointed out to me as the right answer and I can see they are a possible interpretation, but I never would have come to the same conclusion of my own accord, because all I see is a mass of facts, which must follow some great logical web, but it's a web that I can't see.

When man is capable of the funniest, saddest and most exciting acts of imagination, it is hard to be one of the few members of mankind who are forced to read, day in, day out, paragraphs like: "Reasonable financial provision – s.1(2)(b) such financial provision as it would be reasonable in all the circumstances of the case of the applicant to receive for his maintenance."

By the time I wrote this, I had had enough of the hidden magic that filled London's Inns of Court when I had begun studying to be a barrister three years earlier. And the magic truly was hidden.

Although I had lived in central London all my life, I had never been into the squares and streets of Lincoln's Inn, Gray's Inn, Middle or Inner Temple – the four Inns of Court. My bicycle routes round the city had often skirted their walls and railings but I hadn't taken in what hid behind them. Like anybody else, I could have gone in at any time during the day, but the entrances and exits, though sometimes grand, never invited in the passer-by. The entrance for every road had a checkpoint and a guard by it. Even the paths seemed to have been planned to turn at right-angles – it was impossible for an unknowing pedestrian to see a way through to a familiar street on the other side of the Inn and work out how he might get out of these four interconnecting little walled towns.

The few people who did walk in did so with a sense of serious purpose. They had something to do – something that was inevitably law-related – and they were well-dressed to do it. The area was so exclusively associated with law that bits of it were named after legal concepts, like Chancery Lane, as if the dry and arcane practice of Chancery, with its wills, trusts and charity law ("There never was such an infernal cauldron as that Chancery on the face of the earth," Dickens wrote in *Bleak House*), was too powerful to be restricted to these solemn cloisters and had leapt over the walls and into the streets beyond.

Once I worked out that I, like any member of the public, was allowed to stroll through these entrances, I felt a blast of smugness at the knowledge that few non-lawyers ever found their way into the place. Here, just off some of the most crowded streets in London – the Embankment, High Holborn, Fleet

Street — were hushed rows of 17th- and 18th-century houses. Those walking round the place are well-off and, for the most part, not bad-looking. There are no tramps and no children. Very few cars manage to get through the checkpoints, and those that do, go at a gentle five miles an hour in the knowledge that there will be no need to jostle and double-back in the feverish search for parking spaces. All the spaces are reserved: anyone allowed into the Inn will definitely have one waiting for them.

There's very little noise. There are no shops, and practically all the workmen are employed by the Inns and know not to disturb the barristers with radios and chit-chat. Apart from the lawyers' chambers, the Inns are empty: the large medieval gardens, chapels and halls are open only to barristers and, for most of the day, and the year, not even to them.

The magic has been enriched by novelists — Dickens being the chief cult. Even when he was pointing out the horror of the law, how it takes over clients' lives and destroys them, he still injects romance: in *Bleak House*, Miss Flite describes the birds she keeps in her Lincoln's Inn room as "the Wards in Jarndyce. They are caged up with all the others. With Hope, Joy, Youth, Peace, Rest, Life, Dust, Ashes, Waste, Want, Ruin, Despair, Madness, Death, Cunning, Folly, Words, Wigs, Rags, Sheepskin, Plunder, Precedent, Jargon, Gammon, and Spinach!" Miss Flite nicely captures the misery of those trapped by the law but she made it all sound exciting; far more exciting than the low-level horrors she fails to list: tedium, silence, pomposity or humourlessness.

Journalists have helped the collective effort to flatter the legal profession. Fleet Street cuts a line between the two halves of the Inns of Court – with Gray's Inn and Lincoln's Inn above it, and Middle and Inner Temple below it. Such a convenient source of copy has been helpful to lazy writers over the years, particularly if the chief protagonists, the lawyers, could somehow be made to look dashing.

Even a decade after the newspapers have left Fleet Street, newspapermen keep up the charade. Look at page three of the *Daily Telegraph*, the natural slot for sensationalist coverage of any big murder trial. Take in the edited highlights of five hours of court proceedings, filleted down to 1,000 words concentrating on the most gruesome bits of the case. Now compare all that condensed excitement on the page with the faces of the law reporters and newspaper correspondents in court: blank, expressionless eyes fixed on the middle distance. That alchemy – turning boredom into sensation – lures a lot of people into becoming barristers.

The magic gets another boost from the laymen who have done jury service and, again, have seen only the exciting bits – the courtroom confrontations – and, even better, have had a part to play in them. I know because I was one of them, called to do jury service in my mid-20s when my professional life was far from prospering.

After a degree at Oxford, I went into banking and disliked it. Reading about the law in books and newspapers had whetted my appetite. My decision was sealed by a spell of jury service in a criminal court next to Westminster Abbey which shared some of the abbey's architectural grandeur – all Gothic tracery and dark oak docks, perfect for holding Jack the Ripper types before sending them off to the scaffold.

After the months I had spent dealing with the ephemeral movements of the money markets, the long discussions in the jury room over the fate of a criminal – even if he wasn't a Victorian prostitute killer on trial, but a petty thief, a gypsy accused of credit-card fraud in the Marks & Spencer's on Oxford Street – were a real treat.

There was none of the tapping of computer screens that sliced money out of deals between Wall Street bankers selling futures in the bellies of pigs slaughtered in Iowa. Here was life, red in tooth and claw, directly passed from a seamy real-life incident into my hands: man commits burglary, man caught by police, man judged by me in courtroom.

The fact that the gypsy was acquitted by our jury – 11 thought he was innocent, one guilty – and that I was the one who thought he was guilty, didn't stop me thinking I might be an effective lawyer. I had a good degree in ancient and modern history, which for some reason was held up as compatible with a barrister's career. I had a loud, clear voice. I was comfortable in London and, after public school and Oxford, I was used to ancient cloisters packed with men.

I read further about the law, and another lure emerged. The permanent stamp it has left on British history. As a judge, or even as a barrister introducing an argument that could persuade a judge, you might be responsible for changing the law of the United Kingdom by creating a legal precedent. That sort of permanence is granted to only a few people – politicians, perhaps, when they introduce a new law into Parliament, or artists, if they're good enough to leave great works behind them.

Throw in the intellectual content of a barrister's job and the high-flown oratory it demands, and it's no surprise that the law is held in high regard by those who've never done it; so much so that some of them are determined, like I was, to take part.

And there's the money: if you were in a good chambers, within five years of finishing the two-year training course, you could rely on earning around £100,000 a year. If you were really good – a George Carman, say – you could be on a million a year by the time you were 50.

Carman's life appeared to be the ultimate in professional gratification: as well as the fees, there was the drama, the profiles in the papers, and the low, gossipy intrigue of the world of libel and criminal law that he moved in. And yet however low was the world he dipped into – a world of perjurers, such as Jonathan Aitken, and *EastEnders* actresses like Gillian Taylforth administering oral-sex in motorway lay-bys – Carman could float above it all, because of the planet-sized integrity and intellect that barristers are supposed to have. And, so the thinking goes, the integrity and intellect just go on growing and growing if, like Carman, you're a QC. By the time you're made a judge, you're bursting with goodness.

Second only to being Carman, and earning Carman-like quantities of money and fame, would be to work with him. And, in the limited circles of the libel chambers where I was planning to get a job, there was every chance of that happening. With such high expectations, the reality was bound to disappoint. It did not, though, need to be the most soul-destroying job I have ever done.

***

After four years of academic study, or five if, like me, your first degree is not in law, the barrister starts life as a pupil shadowing a senior barrister, or pupil-master, for a year. Pupilmasters are supposed to take pupils under their wings, gently correct their mistakes and show them how it all should be done. More often than not, though, the pupilmaster's job is rotated round a chambers from year to year and is forced on people who do not really want an ignorant shadow around, always asking their pupilmaster what he's up to – which is how pupils are supposed to learn.

I had been chosen in an interview nine months before I actually started. The three barristers who had taken the interview were sympathetic enough. But, once I started the job, no effort was made to match me up with a pupilmaster I might get on with. It was the same, across the board, with my friends from Bar School (the vocational final year of a barrister's training): state-educated pupils were billeted on raging snobs, and attractive women shared rooms with serial adulterers. To deaden the impact of such clashes, an unwritten law has developed: pupils are expected to be seen and not heard. The pupillage system has been going on for 300 years, but things have, if anything, got worse since Dr Johnson's day, when pupils were at least encouraged to speak. In 1750, he wrote in *The Rambler* that the point of the legal training for students was, "to raise themselves from pupillage by disputing the propositions of their teacher".

If I had disputed any propositions with my first pupilmaster, David Frobisher, I'd have been shown the door of my chambers – albeit a fine 18th-century oak-panelled door with plaster scrolls on top of it, framing an Adam-style wrought-iron fanlight.

***

Frobisher made clear from our first meeting that, for the three months I was with him, his propositions were not there to be disputed; and my propositions were to be neither here nor there.

At the beginning of October, I was taken to meet him in his drawing room on the third and top floor of chambers: a low-ceilinged attic room, its mediocrity salvaged by a commanding view over Temple gardens, across the Thames, past the Oxo Tower to the BBC transmitter on top of Crystal Palace Hill ten miles to the south. One of the clerks showed me the way, scurrying ahead of me up the three flights of stairs without a word, before rapping on one of two doors at the top of the house.

That is essentially what all barristers' chambers are – houses which haven't really been converted into offices, just left as drawing room after drawing room after drawing room. The rooms vary only in size: with the biggest on the first floor, the medium-sized on the second, and the smallest at the top. Each barrister is allowed to decorate their room in whatever way they want, although most settle for cream and white or deep red and white. A few go for pictures: classical reproductions, framed posters of Royal Academy exhibitions, that sort of thing. Most, like David Frobisher, kept their walls blank, the cream, white or red only broken up by the brown spines of the bound law reports, which in his case filled an eight foot by six foot cavity opposite the only window – a small, square one – in his attic room.

"Mr Frobisher, this is Harry Mount, your pupil," said the clerk, before slipping out of the room.

I stuck out my hand.

"Hello," he said, his hands firmly stuck to his side.

"Oh, hello." I let my outstretched hand slip to my side as unobtrusively as I could, passing it off as the sort of truncated wave I always made when I met somebody.

"If you sit over there." He pointed to a table and chair wedged into a corner of the room that looked away from the view over the gardens and straight at the wall cavity full of law reports.

And that was it – for the next three months that I shadowed him, we hardly spoke. He hardly ever addressed a single word about the law to me, and his conversation about anything that wasn't connected to the law was virtually non-existent. One such rare interchange occurred on my second day of shadowing him: he bumped into me outside the office on a wet morning. I was wearing a waterproof for my journey into work on a moped.

"Is that a golfing top?"

"Yes."

"What's your handicap?"

"I'm not really good enough to have one."

"Oh."

Later that morning, I got him some coffee. "White – splash of hot milk, plenty of space between the coffee and the edge of the cup, no sugar."

Emboldened by our interchange about the waterproof top, I thought that now was a good time to talk.

"So, David, if you don't mind me asking, what's the plan for the next three months?"

"There isn't one."

"Oh, should I just get on with the paperwork you gave me yesterday?"

"Yes."

"Right. Thanks very much. I'll crack on."

I'd never used the expression "I'll crack on" before. But that was the effect of David's long silences, punctuated with abrupt commands. In trying to strike up conversation with someone who didn't *do* conversation, an imbalance of enthusiasm developed: because there was none on his side, there was too much on mine.

"In court today for the Sellaby case, are we?" I said on our third day, our first in court together, in a contractual dispute over who owned the leases on a series of Cheshire pubs.

"Yes."

"Excellent. Are we going to pull it off?"

I sounded like Joyce Grenfell.

"Up to the judge."

There was no life in his eyes, no reaction at all – apart from a concerted effort to look in any direction other than towards where I was sitting, to show that he wanted me to stop asking questions. The day in court was then spent going through all the documents related to the various pubs and working out exactly where in Cheshire they were, and disputing the leases with David's opponent, Richard Brooke. We ended up winning.

"Right, you'd better get this order to Brooke's chambers," David said, handing me a piece of paper. "No Cheshire cat he."

I laughed as loud as I could. He was also laughing, with his head bowed down over a ring binder. Unlike most people who tell a joke, he felt no need to check that it had gone across well – he would have laughed in exactly the same way if no one had been in the room. Perhaps I should have laughed louder at what was David's first joke in three days; particularly since it turned out to be his only one in three months, apart from the ones he seemed to make to himself as he ploughed through paperwork.

"What's that?" I turned round in my small chair, when I first heard him laugh in this random way.

"Nothing."

He chuckled on, shaking his head in mock

ignorance as he confronted legal problems that he knew he was on the verge of solving.

***

By the end of the third day with David, the routine was set.

"Morning," I would say enthusiastically at 9am.

"Morning," he would usually – though not always – say back to me.

After that, I would spend the day either working through papers and staring at the bookcase full of law reports that was 12 inches from my nose or accompanying him to court.

Going to court was easier to put up with – there were other people around, who were perfectly capable of having a conversation. But court visits were rare: although the spotlight falls on barristers when they are in court, they spend far more time in chambers preparing cases.

"I've got something for you," he would sometimes say first thing, instead of "Morning".

Then he would hand over a set of papers for his new case, photocopied by one of the clerks, give a brief explanation of our position and then go quiet for a week or two, until the case came to court. This only happened in about a quarter of his briefs – the rest were settled out of court or were never meant to go to court in the first place; he was often asked to advise solicitors over the telephone.

"Interesting news, David," were the only words that would command his attention. He didn't want to be asked questions or exchange small talk. The object in the corner of his room – me – was to stay quiet, unless it could be of some active help.

"They've got a judgment in the Riley case," I would say about a trial that might affect David's chances on the case he was working on. "Oh, and the clerks told me they've got copies of those law reports you wanted. I'll go and get them."

"I'll go and get them" was better, I worked out, than the rigmarole of me asking, "Shall I go and get them?", and him saying: "Of course."

Pragmatic statements like this – maybe two or three of them a day – were my limit. Anything more – an anecdote, a joke, or a thought – sounded so awkward and heavy-handed after the silence that had preceded it and the one that followed, that it was impossible to create the sort of relaxed atmosphere where natural, rambling conversation could flow.

Sitting alone in his room all day, David never had to do anything he didn't want to do. He hardly drank, didn't smoke, and had few friends, no children, no girlfriend and minimal family contact. As a result, he had no natural demands on his time other than those made by his stomach and bowels.

"Lunch," he would say at 12.45, before going off on his own, returning at 1.45.

His next words would be, "I'm going home," at around 6.35 in the evening.

Although he never looked at me when I was talking to him, whenever I wasn't talking to him he kept a half-eye on me – any sudden movement upset him.

"Oh God," he shouted on my first morning when I closed the door to his room. "Push the handle down when you close the door."

"Gentle!" he urged, when I put his coffee down next to him. "By the lamp base, on the coaster."

Afterwards, whenever I put his cup down, I made sure it made a gentle "plik" noise, never a hearty "pok".

My experience was common among other pupils.

The isolated world in which barristers moved, except for the rare occasions when they went to court, meant they rarely had to make compromises with anyone other than judges. Otherwise they were only ever among equals or those who were officially thought inferior – clerks and pupils. Even if the barristers' world hadn't attracted in the first place a certain sort of pompous figure, its secluded atmosphere allowed idiosyncrasies to fester.

In surroundings where bullying could develop so easily, it seemed extraordinary that a grown-up person – David must have been around 60 – could be so rude, especially given that he hadn't got the excuse of being stupid. But there was some consolation in the fact that the other members of his chambers clearly didn't find him easy company.

"David Frobisher's your pupilmaster, is he?" said Julian Woodhouse, the oldest member of chambers and the first I was introduced to by the clerks.

"Oh right," he paused, "Excellent mind."

"Oh right," said Francis Garton, the member of chambers responsible for pupils, with a sharp intake of breath. "He'll make you work hard."

The strict hierarchy of chambers meant that no

barrister could be really rude about another one to a pupil. For that, I had to go to a retired judge and writer whom I met a year later at a newspaper party.

"David Frobisher? Complete wanker. You should have complained. We're not all like that, you know. At least I hope we're not!"

The friction between David and me wasn't a case of, as Jane Austen put it in *Emma*, "One half of the world cannot understand the pleasures of the other." He did have some pleasures which I could understand perfectly well, even share; shooting, golf and supporting Liverpool were chief among them. But they were solitary pleasures which needed no understanding of the human condition to appreciate. Anything that involved some interest in the day-to-day activities of human beings was beyond him – I never heard him refer to a book or a film or even a television programme he liked. And he took a distinctly masochistic approach to those pleasures he did indulge in.

"After last night's display, Liverpool have my permission to go out and shoot Michael Owen," he said solemnly of one game.

He never referred to a single social event that he'd

been to, despite his one piece of advice, delivered in a solemn tone, about how I should approach the Bar.

"My oldest friend once said I should work hard and play hard."

He rarely laughed on the phone and even more rarely took personal calls. Although heterosexual and not bad-looking for a man in late middle age – his plumpness hadn't dulled his strong Duke of Wellington features, his thick hair was dyed a deep black – he had never married and had never had children. He didn't feel the lack of family life; the one thing that he did appear to be interested in was money.

"Make sure you do some billable work every day," he said out of the blue one day, jerking his head up from his paperwork for the first time in several hours. "A day spent doing only admin is a day wasted."

But it was hard to be envious of the large amounts of money he earned, when he never seemed to spend it on anything remotely interesting. He had a grand car which he was clearly very proud of: he always climbed into it slightly more slowly than was strictly necessary, presumably hoping that he might be seen by a colleague with a less grand car. But he had no great interest in cars generally, just the one he happened to own, and even then only for the few seconds that somebody else was coveting it.

It wasn't as if he was just one of those vague, other-worldly people who are oblivious to what is going on around them. He was outraged if you behaved for a moment in the same way that he did.

"Look at this," he said one morning, dropping a bundle of documents on to my desk from an unnecessary height with a great thud, "and come up with an answer."

When I came back with a vague answer that went with the vague terms of the request, he insisted that he had made more specific demands of me.

"Well, actually," I said, "I don't remember you asking me exactly that."

He stood up, turned to the window and stared blankly up at the sky, hands folded behind his back.

"Why, when I asked you to do these things, didn't you do them?"

"I'm afraid I just forgot that you gave specific instructions."

"And why did you forget?"

"I'm not sure. Carelessness?"

"It's not very helpful to be careless, is it?"

"No."

In the 13 weeks during which we shared a room, we had one drink together. After work one Friday, we strolled to a wine bar round the corner from chambers, about five minutes away. Because we were involved in a physical activity – walking – and because cars were passing along Fleet Street, providing enough sound to fill the silences, there was little pressure to talk as we made our way to the bar.

We both knew we wouldn't have to be there for very long. When he first made the offer of a drink, he tacked on the condition that he would have to leave early for the country. I also invented an appointment for later that evening, in case he took his time to make a move.

There was a window of about three-quarters of an hour to fill. Talking about what drinks we would have – a glass of champagne each – and talking about champagne in general took a few minutes. The rest of the time passed with me asking him questions about work, all of which he answered in single sentences. Annoyed, I determined not to ask him anything, and instead waited in silence to see what he could come up with.

He said nothing, but I remained resolute, staring into the dark recesses of the bar, rationing my sips of champagne to avoid looking like I was constantly drinking because I had nothing else to do or say.

After about a minute, he spoke.

"Do you play any sports other than golf?"

***

For the rest of my time with David, I tried every single conversational approach possible. I thought he disliked me intensely and, having heard someone say that when people dislike you it's often because they think you dislike them, I thought the best way to get through to him was with an all-out campaign of friendliness.

Because he was so silent, I couldn't just keep on talking. Instead I said the few things I was allowed to say – the "Hello" and "How are you?" every morning – with gusto, raising the pitch of the words so they ended on a high note.

On the few occasions he spoke, I answered with a broad grin on my face. "I'd love to," I bellowed, when he asked me to pick up his printer from the computer repair shop down the road and carry it back to chambers.

"It'd be a pleasure," I cried as I ran to the door and made the trip to St James's to pick up his Barbour from the mender's in time for that week-end's shooting.

But I couldn't go on being friendly in a vacuum. I was perfectly happy to be a servant, but not to a vindictive master. After two months of him not responding, I gave up, leaving me another five weeks of almost complete silence.

Still, however miserable I felt on the inside, I couldn't let it show on the outside. With a year in which to impress as a pupil, a year in which conversation was frowned upon by the pupilmasters, I had to strike a note of silent sycophancy. There wasn't much chance to offer help regularly because the tasks I was given tended to stretch out over weeks – wading through great bundles of papers on a case or taking notes in court of what all the parties were saying – and I was expected to say nothing as I beavered away.

All that I could do, for days at a time, was give out enthusiastic body language: turn pages with brio, then pause for a moment, sit up and look into the middle distance, which I imagined existing somewhere beyond the bookcase full of law reports ahead of me, and then crouch down again and vigorously write something interesting in my notebook.

This charade worked for a while but, in the end, I gave in to apathy – I couldn't keep up the appearance of happiness and energetic usefulness, while being so miserable on the inside. In the early mornings, at the thought of what lay ahead, I fell into a deep melancholy. It wasn't just wistful, low-key sadness. It was waking-up-at-five-o'clock-in-the-morning despair, heart pounding with apprehension at the thought of the humiliating silence I would have to endure through the day, before evening brought the relief of solitude.

This dawn desperation became so regular that I stopped looking at my watch to check what time it was when I woke up. I could then try to convince myself that, after all those hours lying in bed dreading the beep of the alarm clock, when it did finally go off I had only been awake for a few minutes.

There was, in theory, a way out of all this; a chance to get another pupilmaster if you weren't getting on with the original one you'd been given. The Bar Council, the body that disciplines barristers and sorts out their training, acknowledges that tensions are bound to arise out of the pupil–pupilmaster relationship, the last proper form of professional apprenticeship with such constant and intense one-on-one contact. The many affairs and sexual harassment suits that develop are inevitable.

And so the council has established a mentorship scheme. As the retired judge I met – the one who called David a wanker – had said, there was a system where you could take any grievance with your pupil-master to a different barrister in the same chambers, one who had been picked as your mentor at the beginning of the year.

There are of course pitfalls in the system. Why should the senior barrister in charge of the adjudication take the side of a whining novice against someone he had been working with for 20 years and would go on working with till retirement?

What pupil would take the risk? The law is so

oversubscribed that there are more people in legal training at any one moment than there are lawyers. There are two law students for every pupillage. And there are two pupils for every tenancy, the job for life that you're given if the chambers take a liking to you after the year's pupillage. The maths is easy. Why put a black mark against your name by complaining when, in the next room, there might be – as there was in my case – a fellow pupil chasing the same job?

That is, if there are any jobs going in the first place. Lots of chambers don't let on until the last few months of the pupillage whether or not they have a vacancy – and there often aren't any – so you keep on flogging away on the off-chance that there'll be some reward at the end of it all.

***

Because you're tucked away in your room all day, you hardly come across your fellow pupils. Things were better when Thackeray wrote about the system in 1849 – pupils were put together in their own room: "In the pupil-room of Mr Hodgeman, the special pleader, six pupils were scribbling declarations."

Victorian chambers may sound like a factory floor, but at least you worked alongside your equals and could work at becoming friends in the face of the constant threat to any prospective friendship: the fact that your success depended on their failure. This dog-eat-dog – or dog takes other dog's job – scenario loomed menacingly over all our dealings with each other, however often we openly discussed the horrors of it among ourselves with forced, hearty, conspiratorial laughter.

My fellow pupil in David Frobisher's chambers was called Silas Thorburn. Ambitious, but honest enough to admit how awful the whole set-up was, he made for a kindred spirit in our passive fight against our pupilmasters.

And there was an added bonus – Silas was short and wore glasses, and had been educated at state school and a redbrick university. On their own, each of these characteristics wouldn't have counted much against him. Together, they looked like making for a self-destructive combination when it came to deciding who would get tenancy at the end of the year.

One October afternoon, at the beginning of our

pupillages, we were introduced to each other by Alec McArdle, Silas's pupilmaster.

"Hello," I said, sticking out my hand.

"Oh, hello," replied Silas enthusiastically, but he didn't shake my hand. We stood in silence, not wanting to speak until we were spoken to. McArdle slowly made his way out of the room.

"Oh God, I'm sorry about that," said Silas. "Alec insists on not shaking hands."

"Not to worry. Mine's the same."

"Didn't he say why?"

"No."

"Alec says it's an ancient convention. If clients see opposing barristers shaking hands, they think they're conspiring with each other."

"But there weren't any clients around."

"Alec says that doesn't make any difference."

According to Evelyn Waugh, the difference between Americans and the British comes down to the rules of politeness: Americans use them as bridges, to get to know somebody better; the British use them as barriers, to keep people at a distance without offending them. Many barristers use the rituals of the Inns of Court, like the handshake rule, as weapons: "I know this rule and you don't, and you should be punished for not knowing it."

David was so keen to ignore me that he couldn't be bothered to tell me the conventions of the Bar, and just left me to flounder in silence. But even silence was better than the Alec McArdle way. Alec was the worst of all worlds: a bully who loved talking, even if – especially if – he had something horrible to say. So he never missed a chance to remind Silas quite how low down the lawyers' food chain he was.

"You're Silas, aren't you?" McArdle had said to Silas on first meeting him.

"Yes."

"Clearly, you don't know the handshake rule," McArdle had said, before giving Silas the short lecture.

"And there's one other thing you ought to know about me before we spend three months together."

"Oh yes?"

"I've got the biggest cock in Gray's Inn."

"Until now," said Silas.

McArdle said nothing, and gestured Silas into his room. He didn't say anything more that morning. In the afternoon, the two of them went to court and met their client, who was contesting the contents of a will.

"We'll be seeing a master in Chancery today, Tim," McArdle said to the client. "Oh, and this is my pupil, Wart."

"How do you do?" said Tim, offering his hand. The handshake rule didn't stop handshakes between client and barrister. But a more fundamental rule – the don't-make-life-difficult-for-your-pupilmaster rule – meant Silas couldn't put Tim right about his real name.

"How do you do?" said Silas.

"Wart will be shadowing us today, if that's OK, but he won't be interfering at all. Isn't that right, Wart?"

"Yes, Alec."

Silas never tried to joke with McArdle again.

Like murder suspects, Silas and I were kept apart from each other during working hours, squirreled away with our pupilmasters for most of the week. But occasionally we bumped into each other on the way home from work or had a drink together away from the wine bars where Alec and the other barristers gathered. There was no danger of bumping into David – he didn't socialise.

When Silas and I met, our conversation usually came down to exchanging horror stories about our pupilmasters. The anecdotes weren't just for our entertainment; they were consoling – if Silas was having such a bad time, then, surely, he didn't have a better chance of tenancy than me. I was pretty sure that he preferred me sticking to nightmare anecdotes too. It was better, then, not to tell him about the two times David and I had come close to a civilised conversation: when he asked about my golfing top and, later on, when he asked whether I played any sport other than golf.

As well as our own individual disasters, there was the generally hellish world of the Bar for us to commiserate each other over. We discussed the pernickety dress rules for hours. Wearing black gowns and the uncomfortable horsehair wigs – £500 for the full kit, not including your suit – is only the most well-known of many less obvious conventions. What sort of suit you wore was particularly important.

There's a Russian proverb, "At meeting you're

judged by your clothes. At parting you're judged by your wits." In the law you're always judged by your clothes. Even on the hottest summer days, you have to keep your jacket on in all meetings, and the jacket has to be either a double-breasted woollen one or, if single-breasted, accompanied with a matching waistcoat.

Beyond these strictures, there were even tinier details that marked the right suit – tailored, ideally, or, failing that, something off-the-peg with all the hallmarks of a tailored suit.

"Four, two, three, one," David said sternly to me one morning.

"Sorry?"

"Four, two, three, one."

"I don't understand."

"Look at your cuffs."

I looked at the sleeves of my shirt.

"Your suit cuffs."

I did so.

"How many buttons do you have on your cuff?"

"Three."

"And how many should you have?"

"I don't know."

"Exactly. Four, two, three, one. Four buttons: yes, for all suits – two-piece, three-piece, tails. Two buttons: yes, for blazers. Three: thought about it, got it wrong. One – never.

"Oh, and you must be able to undo the four cuff buttons."

"When should you undo them?"

"Never!" David shouted, "Except to show they can be undone."

A few weeks later, in the evening, after a day of complete silence, he looked up at me as I left the room at six to go home.

"What's wrong with the ends of your trousers?"

"I don't know."

"Turn-ups! Trousers must have turn-ups."

***

And so it went on. Shirts must be double-cuffed to allow the use of cuff links, and must never have breast pockets. What could you possibly want to put in a pocket? A bus ticket? Garish colours were allowed in jacket linings, handkerchiefs and, for senior barristers, socks.

Silas had been half-aware of some of these rules when he began pupillage. But he was short of money.

So, to make do, he had hacked off the buttons on the cuffs of his single-cuffed shirt and fashioned some little slits to jam his cuff links into.

"Can't afford a proper shirt?" McArdle shouted at him on his first morning.

"Sorry?"

"You can't just stuff cuff links into a normal shirt."

Silas bought a proper shirt at lunchtime at the best shirt shop in Chancery Lane, cutting his year's budget by a pound a week as he did so.

The strict rules extend to eating. Barristers have to dine 12 times in the Inns' ancient dining halls before they can be called to the Bar. The dinners are held in the evening at 7.15pm and finish at around nine. During the meal, the outside door to hall is shut to stop people coming in late or leaving early, to make sure they don't just show their faces to give the impression that they've dined, and then do a quick about-turn.

I dined in hall for the first time two years before starting pupillage. I went with three people who were doing their legal training with me, so we could form a "mess" of four – a little group sitting, two opposite two, bunched up in a long line of messes on adjoining tables all leading up to High Table, where the judges and benchers of the Inn sat.

"How are you?" I said to the man on the next-door table, who I'd chatted to a bit at Bar School.

"You're not allowed to talk to me, I'm afraid," he said.

"Why not?"

"I'm sorry. I really can't talk to you any more. Or I'll get sconced."

"Why can't I talk to him?" I asked Silas.

"It's a rule," he said, filling up a water glass with cheap red wine.

"What's the rule?"

"No talking to the next-door mess, except to ask for salt, pepper or water."

"What happens if you break it?"

"You're sconced."

"What?"

"Drink this," he said, passing the water glass full of wine to me without any pleasure. "In one."

"Scooooooonce," the other two on our table lowed gently as I drained the glass.

Just as I was putting the glass down, a waitress

came and put four plates in front of me.

"Oh, and you're serving," Silas said.

"What?"

Silas passed a small leaflet to me – "Guide to Dining in Hall". Opening it, he pointed to a small diagram, showing the four members of each mess, marked as A, B, C and D.

"You see," he said, "Everyone sitting in the top left of each four – this one, marked A – has to do the serving. You're top left, so you're A. You serve out the food and order the wine and the extra vegetables The rest of us can't talk to the waitresses."

Just because I was ordering the wine, it didn't mean I had to pay for it; as a gesture to my mess, though, I bought some good claret, making sure that I then asked the others if they'd like, not "some wine", but "some claret" – I wasn't immune to the drip-feed of pomposity that barrister life so relentlessly provides.

Silas and the other two were hardly drinking anything, so I drank about half the bottle.

"Just going to the loo," I said before pudding.

"You can't," said Silas.

"You're joking?"

"Afraid not. Can't leave until the end of the meal."

"I know that. I'm not leaving Hall. I'm just going to the loo."

"That's what I mean. You can't leave the room to go to the loo until coffee's served; and you can't leave Hall altogether until after coffee."

"But I'm absolutely desperate."

"I'm sorry," said Silas, "I couldn't care less... but the beadle could."

"Well, I'm going anyway."

I got to my feet and walked towards the loos beyond the hall's ornate medieval screen. The doors set into the screen were closed. In front of them stood the beadle, a lean man in his late 60s, well turned out in a dark suit and black gown, holding a five-foot-long, gold mace. Smart as he was, he didn't have the look of a senior judge; he had the giveaway air of the long-term Inn servant – with the familiar mix of strict compliance to the Inn's etiquette rules thrown in with a surliness to those who broke them, or looked as though they were going to break them.

"Yes, sir?"

"I wondered if I could go to the loo."

"Yes, sir. When coffee is served."

"Oh, I know the rule. I'm very sorry but I'm desperate."

"I can only let you through if there's an emergency."

"This is a bit of an emergency, actually."

"I can only let you through if there's a proper emergency."

"Couldn't you turn a blind eye?"

"I can only let you through if there's a proper emergency."

I turned and went back to my table, where Silas was filling a large water glass with the cheap red wine – the claret had run out.

"I'm sorry," he said, passing it to me.

"Scooooooonce."

***

Lunch is a less formal affair. You can go to Hall on your own and talk to whoever you want. But it still has its regulations. One day, enjoying a solitary meal in Lincoln's Inn Hall, reading a book propped up alongside my plate, I was interrupted by a waiter.

"Excuse me," he said, a little embarrassed. "I've been asked by a bencher to remind you of the rule against reading books or newspapers in Hall."

I looked up to see a lone purple-faced man at High Table at the other end of the room glaring in my direction. I put my book down and, like the Bencher, set about staring into thin air. A few weeks later, I was asked to leave Inner Temple Hall for reading a newspaper during pudding.

Given that law is supposedly a learned profession – barrister MPs in the House of Commons are still referred to as "the learned member for Garboldisham West" as opposed to "the honourable member" – the halls might be thought of as places where learning is encouraged. They had been originally used for lectures in oratory and legal knowledge, as well as for dining. Plays were also held there – the first performance of *Twelfth Night* took place in Middle Temple Hall in 1602. But somehow rules that militate against self-improvement have crept in to these supposed halls of learning.

"Why aren't you allowed to read in Hall?" Silas asked McArdle one day, at my request. I didn't dare put the question to David – he didn't like me asking questions. McArdle liked being asked questions, so he could get cross answering them.

"What do you want to read in Hall for?"

"Oh, I don't. I just saw somebody being told off for doing it the other day."

"Didn't he fucking know he's not allowed to read in Hall."

"I don't know. Why isn't he allowed to, anyway?"

"Doesn't he have any bloody friends? You're supposed to be talking to other people, not fucking reading."

***

"What does he mean?" I said to Silas, when he reported this back to me. "Most of them are sitting on their own anyway."

"Yes," said Silas, who never went to Hall, "But I bet they're not reading."

"No. They're staring into space and avoiding people they've been avoiding for 50 years."

***

My difficult time with David meant that, when I moved on to my next pupilmaster, Luke Parker, I was like a chimp that had been badly mistreated in my last zoo: I was untrusting, nervous and unforthcoming.

"Coffee," he said, after we had exchanged more

small talk in five minutes than I had in the previous three months with David.

"Oh yes. Sorry. How would you like it?"

"No, I meant 'Coffee?' – would you like some?"

***

Still, the very fact of being in a small room all day – even if it was a nicely panelled 18th-century one – within three yards of a 60-year-old man going through his paperwork – albeit a nice 60-year-old man this time – was just a slightly cooler version of the hell I had lived in before. I was still kept in a confined space in semi-silence, with only a drip-feed of cases about disputed rights of way and clumsily drafted wills – occasionally leavened by a bit of media law, which had a little more human interest – to keep me going for eight hours a day.

Even when Luke was working from home, and I was briefly unhitched from my master, I couldn't leave the building because the clerks, who were all housed together in one room by the front door, kept an eye on the pupils and ensured we stayed there all day.

The clerks occupied a strange slot in the great hierarchy that connected everyone in chambers, all the way down from law lords, through judges, through QCs to junior barristers. There were five or six clerks in every chambers, slotted into a strange position on the ladder. In theory they were at the bottom of it: they were unlikely to be graduates and many of them had left school at 16. But they essentially controlled the barristers' lives, choosing which barristers should do which cases, giving the best briefs to their favourites and the less appetising ones to junior barristers who weren't really allowed to turn them down. Placed above them all was the senior clerk, who took ten per cent of the proceeds of any case: so, if the barristers in your chambers were in the George Carman bracket, senior clerks could rake in £100,000-£200,000 a year.

And yet, it was understood that clerks had to give all the outward signs of being inferior to all the barristers, however young the barristers might be and however little they might earn. Clerks had to address them all as Mr, Mrs or Miss Whatever, while barristers called the clerks by their first name.

Pupils occupied a strange sort of middle ground. On the day they were taken on and became tenants, the clerks would call them Mr/Mrs/Miss Whatever.

But, until then, they were considered to be on the same level as the clerks, who called the pupils by their first name and were curtly polite – there was no point in being friendly to someone who would probably only be around for a year and would never earn them anything. At the same time, it made no sense to be actively hostile to pupils as long as there was a chance that they might be taken on and might one day end up paying the clerks' wages. But, as long as the pupils remained pupils, it was perfectly within the clerks' rights to behave to them exactly as if they were pupils, school pupils: ie, to make sure they didn't arrive late or leave early, and to report any transgression to their pupilmasters.

***

With pupilmaster and clerks acting together as guards, I was under somebody's supervision constantly for a year. The physical obligation to be in one room for hours at a stretch was gruelling. Sometimes I clenched my whole body, desperately willing the day to end. When it all got too much, I made carefully spaced-out visits to the only two places you were allowed to go: the loo and the library. Just moving into a different building – an annexe of the same chambers, still in the Temple – for the second six months of my pupillage, was a relief for my eyes and ears, bored as they were of fixing on the same stationery cupboards, the same partners' desks, and the same creaks on the same stairs.

My pupilmaster there, Simon Griffiths, was a positively kind man. Whenever I did anything helpful, he often said "Kindness" instead of thank you, which gave me a little lift on particularly miserable days.

Despite his gentle qualities, though, he was still on a different wavelength.

"Bit of a low moment last night," I said to him one morning.

"Oh really?"

"Yup. I went to pick up my moped from Gray's Inn and someone had painted 'dickhead' in lipstick on the seat."

"Oh, poor you. Why?"

"I think I'd parked it badly and they couldn't get their motorbike out."

"God, how horrible. Have you told the police?"

"Oh no. I just thought it was quite funny."

I wanted him to laugh. He thought I was bleating.

The confusion was typical of our dealings together – always slightly failing to connect, so that comments on both sides had to be shorn of all irony. Everything had to be left as bald statements of fact.

Everywhere else in life – school, university, marriage, at parties – you can choose from a pool of people who you really would like to spend time with. And, if someone is nice but no more than that, you can quickly move on from them. But not at work; and particularly not in pupillage.

Still, there's no suggestion that the system should be changed. There's some fiddling around at the edges, with the introduction of the mentors, and a professional education programme, which involves a week's training devoted to accounting and good practice, but essentially the pupilmaster system – and the bullying endemic within it – hasn't changed since the pupilmaster system got going over 300 years ago. Milton saw the system in much the same light that I did. "I hate a pupil teacher, I endure not an instructor that comes to me under the wardship of an overseeing fist."

And when it came to the other barristers in my chambers, there was little consolation. Even as the full horrors of pupillage grew clearer with the passing of the first few weeks, I clung to the consolation that there would be a better world at the end of it all – the George Carman world – where all my intellectual and financial needs would be met.

But in those same first weeks, I was beginning to realise that pupillage was not some baptism of fire, a test of chivalry by social exclusion, after which you would be brought into a warm fold of brilliant minds, heartily slapped on the back by a circle of new welcoming friends. In fact, most of the barristers were cold not only to me, but to each other.

At four o'clock every day, there was chambers tea, when all the barristers who were in chambers that afternoon gathered in the largest room in the building. It was supposed to be a social occasion, when people could tell each other what they had been up to during the day.

On my first day, after a morning of silence with David in his room, followed by a quiet lunch in a sandwich bar on my own, I had grown quite unused to talking in daylight hours. But, when the clock over the mantelpiece in David's room struck the first of four chimes and he shot up from his desk, murmuring "Tea", I was determined to make an effort. I followed David down to the largest room in the building, two floors below him on the chambers' *piano nobile*, where another clock on the mantel-piece was just sounding its fourth chime.

The room was occupied by Julian Woodhouse, the longest serving member of chambers and the first I'd met at the beginning of my pupillage. Now in his early 70s, he was still acknowledged as the world's leading expert on rights of way and came into work every day to see what developments were taking place in the field. He had been working on the second edition of his book on an abstruse aspect of the subject for almost a decade – an aspect so abstruse that the only known copy of the first edition was in the author's room.

Julian sat in his chair behind his desk between the two long Georgian windows which looked west along the river towards the Savoy and the Shell building. His chair faced back into the room.

Next to the bookcases which led along the edges of the long room all the way back to the door were seven other barristers, six men, and one woman, who, I had discovered, was called Sara Cartwright, and one pupil – Silas – all standing, all with their heads bent over cups of tea held in their right hands across their chests. All of them were silent. Four more barristers slipped into the room after David and me, some of them a good 20 seconds after the last chime of the clock.

"Hello," said David, as he entered the room.

"Hello, David," they all said.

"Hello," I said.

The silence continued for a minute or so.

"How's the book coming along?" said McArdle to Woodhouse. Silas stood silently by McArdle's side.

"Not bad, not bad. Case going well, Alec?"

"Judgment expected by the end of the week, Julian."

And then more silence, interrupted only by eating and drinking noises, as the 14 of us wolfed down our biscuits and forced hot tea through our throats before it had time to cool down. Once this had been done, we filed out of the room at ten-second intervals, leaving only Julian sitting in his chair. David and I climbed the two flights of stairs up to his room. He closed the door gently as the silent figures of Silas and Alec walked by to their room.

"Don't ever do that again."

"Sorry. What?"

"Speak during tea," he said. "Pupils aren't allowed to. Silas didn't feel the need to say anything, did he?"

"No. It won't happen again. Sorry."

Having been a shy child, it had taken me 20 years to work out how to fill silences, and not rely on someone else to take up the burden. Unlearning all this was easier, and, once the pressure to make conversation had been forcibly removed, tea became a relaxed affair. There was even an illicit pleasure in watching a group of people, who had known each other for 40 years, struggling to come up with something to say. Because I was under no obligation to talk – or, more to the point, was expressly forbidden from doing so – I got the thrill of the observer with none of the hell of being a participant, as if I was watching it all on television. I began to see how restful it must be working as a waiter at an awkward party. For the second six months of my pupillage, when I was no longer expected to go to tea because of the walk from the annexe to the main building, I ended up rather missing it.

For international people-watchers, chambers tea is a useful illustration of how Englishmen prefer to conduct their lives through actions rather than words, that convention is all: the esteem they win in return for what they do comes before acting on the impulses of what they feel. Brilliant as the members of chambers were at the practice of law, they showed no particular interest when it came to talking about it – they would have become plumbers if plumbing had been the best paid and most respected of all jobs.

The law may be mostly devoted to human misery – every case needs an injured party and one that's done the injuring. But that does not mean that the practitioners of law should necessarily be miserable. If anything, it should have the opposite effect – there's nothing so enjoyable as other people's misfortunes. The fact that lawyers occasionally sort out these misfortunes might even inject their lives with a sort of crusading zeal.

But when the lawyers at tea did talk about work, they were unable to distinguish the interesting things about it from the dull – they might as well have been talking about plumbing. It was like an awkward party, permanently on its first drink. The conversation would have died altogether if they hadn't had half-a-dozen life-saving questions in their armoury: "How's the case going?"; "Any good cases coming up?"; "Do anything last night?"; "Do anything interesting at the weekend?"; "When are you going on holiday?"; and "How was your holiday?"

Conversations were exchanges of short speeches: question and reply, question and reply. There was no prospect of the gradual creation of in-jokes that normally grow out of a group of people forced to work in the same building for years, or of anecdote encouraging anecdote, or of the development of fantasy visions built on ideas casually thrown out over tea or a drink.

Anything along those lines, and suspicions of eccentricity or megalomania would begin to spread. The few times the conversation moved beyond law, it had to be stopped from going too far in any direction. The barristers were like crack German spies, sleepers planted in England in their early teens, and told to infiltrate the legal profession. Adept as they were at talking about all things legal, they never dared stray off the topic for fear they would blow their cover. Reading about anything other than law was a particularly dangerous activity – a holiday activity to be confined to the beach or the aeroplane, like playing with a beach ball or buying duty free.

"I went to the Aubrey Beardsley exhibition yesterday," said Luke, at tea one Monday afternoon.

"At the V&A?" said Dominic Burney, another junior barrister. "Wonderful, wasn't it?"

"Yes. I'd only ever seen the odd illustration before. Really lovely – a sort of mixture of cartoons and something by someone like, I don't know... Raphael?"

"Yeah," said Dominic, now putting on a joke voice a bore's nasal whine – to fend off the charge that he was being pretentious by talking know-ledgeably about something other than law. "It's a bit of the old neo-Renaissance thing, innit?

"Oh yeah," continued Dominic, adopting a cod cockney voice. "It's Pre-Raphaelite meets Michelangelo sort of thing."

The room went quiet for ten seconds.

"How's the book going, Julian?" said Alec.

***

Despite all these years spent together in a situation ripe for comedy, a situation that has in fact been used as a setting for countless comedies – courts, wigs, crooks being sued, the ripped-off doing the suing – barristers didn't take the risk of being funny.

Jokes were restricted to the pompous sending-up of pomposity. Chatting to Silas in Alec's room – Alec was away – and flicking through the shelves, I came across a book that had fallen down the back and had come to rest behind a set of law reports. It was the first edition of Julian Woodhouse's book on rights of way; the only time I had seen a copy outside Woodhouse's room.

On the flyleaf, Julian had written, "To Alec McArdle, a real *amicus curiae*." This was a legal term, meaning "friend of the court" – an impartial adviser in court. In the *Pickwick Papers*, Dickens also used the expression, of a pompous lawyer talking to a friend – "I shall be happy to receive any private suggestions of yours, as *amicus curiae*." Julian's dedication continued, "I hope you enjoy it. I use the term 'hope' advisedly, on the express understanding that you will not sue me for breach of promise if you find it's not up to scratch."

The barristers' awkward behaviour was brought into focus by the daily glimpses I got of normal life outside the walls of the building. A few feet beyond the window of my room in the Inner Temple, builders were renovating an old office building. It lay outside the bounds of the Inn, so they weren't as quiet as the builders who worked inside the Temple's walls.

With chambers being so quiet, the builders' comments were often the only spoken English I heard all day. They never had conversations as such. Instead there were rapid bursts of one-sided talk, which were often no more than catchphrases from television programmes. *The Harry Enfield Show* was particularly popular at the time. "You didn't want to build that fucking wall like that, did you?" I heard the foreman shout at the most junior builder on the site.

Over time, I worked out their names: the foreman was called Tony, the junior builder, Don. If they weren't quoting from television or going through the plotline of a particular programme, they were happy enough firing brief insults at each other or shouting at the radio.

"Leave it out, geezer," Don shouted at Chris Tarrant early every morning whenever the disc jockey got particularly enthusiastic. "Some of us have got hangovers."

Even without any proper conversation as such, the talk was non-stop. If there was nothing to get cross about, a few of the builders resorted to exaggerating their bodily functions, burping loudly and congratulating themselves for it.

"Atchooah," Don would cry every time he sneezed, enunciating each letter.

Because there was very little two-way interchange, room for developing in-jokes was limited. So they contented themselves with their own little turns. Don turned out to be the chief joker. He was instantly recognisable because of his rasping, deep, confident voice and because of his donkey impression – "Hee-haw, hee-haw" – which he did whenever he was forced to do anything menial. This happened often, because he was at the bottom of the pecking order.

"I told you to get that fucking sand an hour ago," said Tony one long afternoon, when Luke was out of the room and I had been busy for several hours making neither head nor tail of a property-developing deal in Surrey.

"Hee-haw, hee-haw."

The foreman did a vigorous wank-off sign.

"Stop making hand signals," said Don, adopting an upper-class accent but retaining the deep and husky edges to his voice, sounding like a hungover, 60-a-day duke taking a domestic to task.

Whenever an architect left the building site, Don did the duke impersonation again.

"How are you today, my dear sir?" he would say, wheeling a barrow of plaster fragments up the plank that leant against the skip, tilting it in the direction of Tony who was mixing concrete just below him, so that the plaster shifted to the edge of the barrow but never quite spilled over.

Despite the swagger, Don was ultimately aware of his position. "I'm just a house-basher," he said, when the architect congratulated him on an awkward bit of plasterwork during a tour of inspection.

In the flesh, the builders rarely matched up to the characters I had mentally sketched on first hearing them. I had imagined Tony, the hard-swearing Scottish foreman, as the sort of old thug whose vanity and anger kept him thin and black-haired – he turned out to be grey and obese.

It was a long time before I saw Don. All I could see was the roof of the building he was working beneath; so I could only go on the flow of his wisecracks from the window below. After several months, I glimpsed him for the first time, working on the roof outside for the first time. With his old-fashioned name and croaky voice, I thought he would be a spare, tubercular, prematurely aged, Artful Dodger type.

When I saw him, he was striding along the duckboards on the roof whistling, like an optimistic plump dwarf on a catwalk. It was a shock to see someone who, his wide girth apart, was so small and young – he looked about 14 – that it seemed he wasn't fully grown yet.

Because the builders' brittle repartee consisted almost entirely of a mixture of mock insults and quips, it slipped into straightforward abuse with little difficulty. There was an Indian among them, who rarely spoke. Whenever he said something, it was invariably polite and work-related: "I've done the attic," or "I'll get the cement." He didn't join in with the banter of the other workers.

"You haven't understood a fucking thing I've said, have you?" Tony shouted at him one day in response to some question from the Indian that I hadn't heard. It seemed unlikely that the reason why the Indian hadn't understood Tony was, as Tony implied, because his English wasn't up to it – he sounded strikingly more educated than all the other builders.

The builders were often nasty to each other like this. Even more often, practically always, in fact, their conversation was mindless. One morning, at about 11am, I sat and listened to Don and Tony on their coffee break.

"You cunt, Tony, you got biscuits."

"Yeah, and you're not fucking having any."

"Look, who's here," said Don, as he saw someone come in through the main site gate. "It's Mark and, guess what, he's fucking late."

"Oh, fuck off," said Mark.

And so it went on. Like goldfish, they seemed to have a five-second attention span. They never referred to the past, or to the future. All they did was comment on the tiniest incident that was going on at that moment – "You stupid cunt, Don, you've spilt coffee all over your trousers" – and frame it with "cunt" and "fuck", using "fuck" in plenty of its different cognates, the most popular being "fuck", "fuck*ing*" and "fuck*er*".

Once, at the end of the working day, Tony's wife dropped off their son, who looked about eight, at the site.

"Come to check up on the husband, have you, Suse?" said Don.

"Nope," said Suse. "Introducing him to his son."

"Lovely to have him about," said Don.

On Suse's arrival, all the builders stopped swearing. Once she'd driven off, they still refused to swear in front of Tony's son. A shy, plump boy, he shadowed his father round the building site, clutching three videos in his hand.

"What you got there?" said Don.

"*Lord of the Rings, Harry Potter* and *Honey, I Shrunk the Kids*."

"What's your favourite?"

"I haven't seen *Honey, I Shrunk the Kids*. But I love *Lord of the Rings*."

"Me too. Absolutely fantastic," said Don. "A

friend of mine's got a job on the next one. Says it's even better."

"Oh, brilliant. When's it coming out?"

"Don't know. Sometime next year."

In the whole of my six months listening to the builders, this was the closest any of them came to a proper conversation, with a bit of question and answer, anecdote, personal knowledge and references to the past and the future.

They were like the more difficult barristers at tea, not really at ease in their fellow man's company, and battered into a form of civilised exchange only by the presence of something unusual: in their case, a woman or a child; in the barristers' case, a judge.

However mindless the builders were, though, they were more human – less cautious, less calculating, more instinctive – than the barristers. There was always noise – whether it was singing or abuse. There was none of the seriousness and the stolid refusal to respond and, above all, none of the heavy awkwardness, which were the hallmarks of barristers' conversations. And, however fragmented their interchanges, the builders were always trying to amuse each other, even if they then stamped all over each other's efforts. Some of the lawyers saw jokes as diversions at best, annoying at worst.

One lawyer in particular. Just as Tony's son was embarking on a short résumé of *Honey, I Shrunk the Kids*, David Frobisher came into my room in search of a book.

"Dreadful film," he said, overhearing the boy through the open window.

"Quite agree," I said. "I much prefer the French original."

"What?" said David, scanning the bookshelves.

"*Chérie, j'ai diminué les enfants.*"

"Never saw it."

"No, it was a joke."

David took a book from the shelf and, without a word, left the room.

What made it worse was that the barristers were perfectly capable of being polite if they wanted to be. In fact they were more aware of the rules of politeness than most people whenever they talked to another barrister. And when they were addressing judges, they were positively unctuous. But in front of pupils they delighted in breaking the rules.

Nothing the barristers valued – money, social

standing, professional status – was lost by being rude to pupils. And a lot of energy was saved: it may take only ten face muscles to smile and 42 to frown, but it presumably takes none at all just to leave your face in uninterested repose, as David did in my company. I suppose he wasn't really being rude specifically to me, even when he was, incidentally, being rude to me. He was just being rude to a type – he would have been like that to anyone in a pupil's position.

Perhaps it was how we would all behave if we removed from our lives the desire to be liked. Not having to cater to what the other person wanted to hear, or to listen to and answer apt questions, had led to the state of mind where all that mattered were the things David wanted – a white coffee, splash of hot milk, plenty of space between the coffee and the edge of the cup, no sugar; a repaired Barbour that I was to accept from the cleaners only if the tear below the left breast had been invisibly mended; complete silence – and the quickest way to getting what he wanted, by abrupt authority.

The less imaginative barristers were delighted to find themselves at last in the Japanese businessman's ideal world – where professional excellence was all that mattered; where saying "Hello" in the morning was neither here nor there.

But even if you didn't need attractive qualities like charm and humour to get on in this professionals dreamworld, surely you needed it for the outside world when it came to things like making friends and procuring girlfriends and wives?

Well, not really. David seemed to survive perfectly well without friends and, if he had happened to need some, he could always have picked them from his pool of work colleagues. As for marriage, it was striking how that could be sorted out through professional excellence as well: a lot of barristers were married to other barristers, and often from the same chambers.

"If you want to be happy for the rest of your life, marry a divorce barrister," said Silas when we were discussing his pupilmaster, Alec McArdle, who, unappetising as he was, had remained married to his family-lawyer wife for 30 years. "You can be horrible. You can beat them up... have affairs... They'll never divorce you."

"Presumably they could stitch you up beautifully."

"Yup. And all very cheaply," said Silas, who had done a mini-pupillage – a week's work experience – during a university holiday with a chambers specialising in family law (and that mostly means divorce). "But they also know what a disaster divorces always are. No money left, children who hate you, and zero chance of finding someone better. And every chance of going through it all again if you think you have found someone better."

***

This always-look-on-the-dark-but-pragmatic-side of-life approach, this love of professional seriousness over knockabout flippancy, fed its way into the lives of those who worked alongside the barristers. And the deeply rooted black seam of seriousness ran throughout the year.

At Christmas, when my time with David was coming to an end and I had a week off over New Year, my gloom lifted for a bit. At least it did until I opened my one work-related Christmas card – from a solicitor I had chatted to in court a few weeks earlier. The card had a robin on it, in a wig and gown, sitting on an ice-bound fountain in the main quadrangle of a snow-covered Lincoln's Inn. "Merry

Christmas and successful New Year," wrote my solicitor friend. Whatever happened to "*Happy* New Year"? Too frivolous?

Maybe it was naïve to expect anything but seriousness out of a legal career, but surely it wasn't too much to expect it to be interesting. That's the impression that Charles Dickens and the newspapers had given, after all.

During my law studies, I could see that if everything came together, and fine minds bumped into exceptional cases, the law could be fascinating. There was something impressive about the ability of the best judges to build up a body of common law, which gave a set answer to every situation, however quirky – like the case of *Fagan v Metropolitan Police Commissioner* [1969]. Fagan, told by a policeman to park by the kerb, accidentally stopped with his front offside wheel on the constable's left foot.

When the policeman told him to reverse, Fagan said, "Fuck off, you can wait," and turned off the ignition.

Clearly Fagan was up to no good, but he had a point when appealing against his conviction for assault: he maintained that the initial driving on to the foot was unintentional and therefore not an assault, and that his refusal to drive off was not an act capable of amounting to an assault.

The presiding judge, Mr Justice James, was in a bit of a pickle. In order to convict someone of a crime, you have to prove both an *actus reus* – a guilty act – and a *mens rea*: a guilty mind. Here there was an accidental act (driving on to the foot), separated from the later moment when the guilty mind developed (Fagan deciding not to reverse).

Mr Justice James worked out a clever and, like so many judges' rulings, hard to follow – way of dismissing Fagan's appeal. He linked the accident with the evil intent that came after it, making the whole incident one long act: "There was an act constituting a battery which at its inception was not criminal because there was no element of intention, but which became criminal from the moment the intention was formed to produce the apprehension which was flowing from the continuing act."

R v Lamb [1967] was an even trickier case. Lamb, with no intention of doing any harm, pointed a revolver at his best friend, who also thought there was no danger, and encouraged Lamb to fire. Lamb knew that there were two bullets in the gun and that neither of them was in the chamber opposite the barrel. What he didn't know was that, by firing the gun, the chamber moved round one notch, placing a bullet opposite the barrel. Lamb fired and the friend died. Lamb was convicted of manslaughter.

Where a man in the street would call Fagan a crook, he would hardly do the same for Lamb. There's something immediately unfair in treating an accident – what's more, an accident that had been encouraged by the victim – as a criminal offence.

On appeal, the presiding judge, Mr Justice Sachs, worked deftly to acquit Lamb and, at the same time, to manufacture a hard legal principle that, when clinically applied, would always come up with a resolution to such unfair disasters, however idiosyncratic.

He held that, for the act to have been unlawful, there must be "a technical assault" and that for such an assault to take place, the victim must apprehend the immediate application of unlawful force to his body. In this case, the friend, a willing participant in the act, didn't apprehend any injury and so Lamb got off.

A similarly tortuous but ultimately convincing justification was made for the verdict in *DPP v Morgan* [1976]. A husband asked several friends to have sex with his wife, after he thought she had been unfaithful to him. He said to them that she might put up a struggle but that they should ignore this; that was how she increased her pleasure.

In the House of Lords, Lord Simon held up the conviction of the friends with the analogy: "It would hardly seem just to fob off a victim of a savage assault with such comfort as he could derive from knowing that his injury was caused by a belief, however absurd, that he [the victim] was about to attack the accused" – ie, the defendants' belief in the victim's consent had to be based on reasonable grounds. In this case, those grounds weren't reasonable.

Rape is also not excused if the victim submits willingly but as a result of fraud: the defendant in *R v Williams* [1923], a singing master, did not get away with intercourse with one of his 16-year-old pupils by convincing her that sex was good for breathing. Nor did the defendant in *R v Flattery* [1877], who convinced his victim that he was performing a surgical operation. Nor did Mr Elbekkay, in *R v Elbekkay* [1995], who managed to persuade his sleepy and drunk victim that he was her boyfriend.

To catch out the anomalous, it is necessary to define crimes very precisely which, when it comes to sexual crimes, produces its own sort of salacious fascination. In order for a rape to take place, for example, all that's needed is the slightest degree of penetration of the vagina or the anus. So, to quote one of the leading textbooks, *Criminal Law*, by Professor C.M.V. Clarkson of Leicester University and H.M. Keating of Sussex University, "The rubbing of the entrance to the vagina with the penis causing ejaculation is not rape, nor is oral sex (fellatio). Similarly, penetration of the vagina or anus with inanimate objects is not rape. In such circumstances, indecent assault is frequently charged."

As well as being gruesomely interesting, sex crimes and murder give a useful insight into society. Men are overwhelmingly more likely to be homicide victims and killers. Seventy per cent of homicide victims in 2000/01 were male and 86 per cent of persons indicted for homicide were male. Of all groups, children of under one year are most at risk of homicide: four times as many were killed in 2000/01 as there were victims in the 16-30 age group.

Homicide victims are very likely to have known the killer: in the same year, 71 per cent of women victims were killed by people they knew; 59 per cent of them were current or former husbands, cohabitants or lovers, and 28 per cent of them were other members of their family, more often than not their parents. Almost half of all killings were as a result of arguments; only one in ten were committed for theft or gain.

The law also throws an interesting light in the way society changes. In 2001/02, 9,008 female rapes and 735 male rapes were recorded. In 1947, there was a total of 240 rapes of either kind. Violence had increased in the half-century in between, but so had a willingness to report rapes, and the way rapes are recorded had also changed: until 1995, when the legal definition of rape was changed, male rape could not be recorded.

Some of these changes are astonishingly recent. It was only acknowledged in 1949 that rape within marriage was a legal possibility. Until then, the law was as Sir Matthew Hale had put it in 1736 in his *History of the Pleas of the Crown*:

> The husband cannot be guilty of a rape committed by himself upon his lawful wife, for by their mutual matrimonial consent and contract the wife hath given herself in this kind unto her husband, which she cannot retract.

Even as late as 1984, in *R v Caswell*, it was held that pulling one's wife's head on to one's penis was an assault if done against her will, but that forcing her to commit fellatio was not an offence because husbands were incapable of indecent assault.

Trying to nail down general principles to accommodate the peculiarities of human behaviour can be a real art. And the connection made between principle and case can be so artful and tenuous that it cannot remain intact for decades, as the moral framework of society shifts.

Scholars now think that the leading case on cannibalism, *R v Dudley and Stephens* [1884], might be decided differently now. A group of sailors adrift at sea for weeks on end survived by eating the cabin boy. Could they claim the defence of necessity? At the time, no, and the sailors were hanged. If it ever happens again, they would probably be acquitted.

These, though, are the peaks of a thousand years of legal history, the exceptions to the rule. And "the rule" is the endless interpretation of run-of-the-mill cases – the vast majority of those that reach court – in the light of all those one-off cases that together build up the common law.

Lawyers are mostly upmarket administrators, making sure all the correct papers are in court, the right witness statements are in place, the right precedents are followed and the right facts arc brought before the court in the right order to give the most favourable impression of their clients.

The law of rights of way and joint tenancies is not designed to entertain, but the grind should have been a little less torturous in the field I had first been drawn to – libel and media law – but ended up only dabbling in because my chambers specialised in commercial and land disputes.

Libel and media law should have had a more artistic element than, say, divorce or banking law. But dealing with the law of films, newspapers and history books is not the same as dealing with films, newspapers and history books.

Despite the number of libel cases that hit the papers, hardly any of the great bulk that get on to barristers' desks are about the famous and the brilliant. Most of the three months I spent with my last pupilmaster were concentrated on a man who wanted to build a motorbike scrambling course on the southern edges of London, and had been called a vandal – by a local Croydon newspaper.

Jobs are only likely to be entertaining or inter-esting if they're aimed at providing entertainment or interest. Being an actor or a novelist or a deep-sea diving instructor has every chance of being enjoyable – people like watching films and reading books and going deep-sea diving. If a job isn't supposed to provide pleasure, it's unlikely to be pleasurable. The joyless jobs are, though, more likely to be necessary. The world needs lawyers more than it needs deep-sea divers. Accountants are more useful than novelists, cleaning ladies than actors. But there's no earthly reason why being necessary should mean being enjoyable.

About halfway through my pupillage, I went to see the film, *Dead Poets' Society*. One passage stood out from the otherwise indifferent dialogue. Mr Keating, the teacher played by Robin Williams, confronts a philistine pupil who is bored in his class:

> I see that look in Mr Pitt's eye, like 19th-century literature has nothing to do with going to business school or medical school. Right? Maybe.
>
> Mr Hopkins, you may agree with him, thinking, "Yes, we should simply study our Mr Pritchard and learn our rhyme and meter and go quietly about the business of achieving other ambitions." I have a little secret for ya.
>
> Huddle up. Huddle up! We don't read and write poetry because it's cute. We read and write poetry because we are members of the human race. And the human race is filled with passion.
>
> Medicine, law, business, engineering, these are all noble pursuits, and necessary to sustain life. But poetry, beauty, romance, love, these are what we stay alive for. To quote from Whitman: "O me, O life of the questions of these recurring, of the endless trains of the faithless, of cities filled with

the foolish. What good amid these, O me, O life? Answer: that you are here. That life exists, and identity. That the powerful play goes on, and you may contribute a verse." ..."That the powerful play goes on, and you may contribute a verse."

The Robin Williams character isn't quite right. Lawyers are not really necessary to sustain life. They aren't essential in the way that doctors, builders, electricians and plumbers are; but they run them a close second. Law is one of the great and necessary disciplines of a civilised society. And it most certainly is a discipline. Its very nature means that it must squeeze the life out of anything amusing or disturbing and produce dry principles, which are unlikely to be salacious or moving. The point of law is never to entertain, even if it is inadvertently entertaining when entertaining figures like Lord Archer or Mohamed Fayed are brought within its serious halls. The law's aim is to strip everything of its extraneous parts – say, in a pop-music case, the enjoyable bits – and reduce it to its bare bones, to form a precedent for future cases.

In 1993, George Michael took his record

company, Sony, to court because he thought they were pushing him too hard in their demands for further albums. It was an entertaining case that got a lot of press coverage. The newspapers could go into all the familiar hits he had produced under the contract, and the difficulties in the recording studio behind the scenes. The case gave the papers a chance to go through the details of all the money that Michael had earned and the things he had bought with it.

But as far as a lawyer is concerned, all that mattered was that the plaintiff couldn't get out of what he considered an unfair contract. And now, once the principle was in that stripped-down bare form, it could be applied to a million other not very interesting cases – a tree-surgeon, say, contracted out to lop so many oaks, who tries to stop his lopping early because the contracting party, he maintains, had not told him that the oaks were particularly dangerous.

***

"Literature is mostly about having sex and not much about having children," wrote David Lodge. "Life is the other way around."

The same sort of thing goes for the literature of law: it's mostly about the bloodiest bits of a trial. Real legal life is mostly about the dreariest bits that happen before the trial begins, that are more often than not about trying to stop the trial going ahead altogether.

In, say, a trust case or a banking dispute, the juicy questions will be things like: do the two parties hate each other? How often have they been unfaithful? Or how much money have they got? These are the questions that novelists and television directors focus on. They are not the questions that a judge will be interested in going into.

A day that would never have made it into a television director's final cut would be the one I referred to in a diary entry in the opening passage of this book. It was in the August of my pupillage year – only two months to go until it was over; but also, ten months since I had started, and I still knew next to nothing.

The High Court on the Strand had closed for the summer and the Temple itself had practically closed down too. It seemed that the whole of the Bar had decamped to Norfolk or Tuscany; the whole of the

Bar, that is, except for my nice, childless, final pupilmaster, Darius Glover, who had no obligations to anyone and, in the absence of any obligations, preferred working to anything else. In his early 40s, good-looking and helpful, he could in theory have been The Man Who Got Me Interested In Law if he'd been my first pupilmaster. But even with Darius's engaging, languid manner, it was hard to concentrate the mind fully on the documents he had laid out in front of him.

"It's really quite riveting," Darius said, as I leant over his shoulder to get a look at a map of some Leicestershire farmland. "Now Mr Topham, who lives in the farmhouse and owns most of the land on here, is the legal owner of Gunston Field, the one in dispute. But he's neglected it for years; hasn't been near it, even, at his own admission. Twenty-five years ago, the two neighbours – who we represent – put their sheep in there and so, they say, have 'informally taken it over for grazing'. Anyway, Mr Topham Senior has now died, and Mr Topham Junior wants to get his hands on Gunston Field. Have we got a chance, Harry? Go and have a look and give me an answer on Thursday."

I tried. God, how I tried. After several days' work in the library, head buried in law reports till late in the night on Tuesday and Wednesday evenings, looking for precedents and studying the relevant laws, I came up with a rock-solid answer, neatly typed up on ten pages of foolscap.

***

Our clients, the two neighbours, had the right to the place, was my considered opinion.

"Morning, Darius, here it is," I said, when he came into chambers ten minutes after me on Thursday morning.

"Oh, thanks," he said, taking it from me and speed-reading it immediately. He flicked through the pages, at ten seconds a page.

"I'm sorry, Harry," he said, looking up. "Under proportionality stakes, my own view is that our case isn't justified."

Ally McBeal never gets to say things like that. And I wish she would. If I'd heard the expression a few more times, I might have had a better chance of working out what on earth Darius meant.

***

What really occupies the lawyers is not the

sensationalist stuff of fiction, but land disputes like the Tophams', or procedural questions – such as, can we get a preliminary injunction, or apply for a summons to have part of a defence struck out, or what about freezing the defendant's assets abroad as well as in Britain?

And – again unlike the picture as it appears on telly – these sorts of questions are rarely fought out in court rooms, and never in front of juries, but in a series of small rooms at the back of the Royal Courts of Justice, known as the Bear Pit, where masters in Chancery sit on their own with just a barrister from each side for company.

On the rare occasions I came across a good human saga of greed and fame, it soon became concealed in a mass of precedents and procedural law. On a mini-pupillage in a media chambers several years before I started as a pupil, I was invited to sit in on a discussion about a "high-profile" case. I came in late, long after the beginning of the discussion, or conference as it's known in legal circles. I slipped into a seat in the corner, as our barrister, Giles Wilkins, talked away to an outside lawyer called Anthony.

"So what are we going to do to enforce confidentiality?" said Anthony.

"Well, there's no way of enforcing it. They can just go ahead and do it again. There's going to be no way of getting an injunction. All we can go for is punitive damages, but we'll never get what you're looking for."

This went on for an hour or so, with words like "confidentiality" and "injunction" flying around, but no reference to who exactly these high-profile people involved in all this were.

On the way out, I asked Giles whose confidentiality was being breached.

"You sat there all that time and you didn't know? Margaret Thatcher. Anthony's from the *Sunday Times* – he's absolutely spitting blood: another paper printed extracts from her memoirs last weekend and it was supposed to be an exclusive."

***

The famous names, though, were neither here nor there. Lady Thatcher might just as well have been a town councillor from Bridlington writing her memoirs in the *Bridlington Gazette* for all it mattered when it came to things like injunctions and

94

confidentiality. Names didn't matter; principles did.

The most notorious case I witnessed was *Hamilton v Fayed* during that same mini-pupillage. I was lucky enough to sit in on the days when George Carman was in court defending Mohamed Fayed, even though it had only got to the pre-trial hearing stage, before the jury was sworn in – libel is the only legal field, apart from crime, where juries are used. Because other members of the chambers where I was doing my mini-pupillage were representing Neil Hamilton and Mohamed Fayed in junior capacities, I could sit with their pupils near the front of court.

My three days in court gave me a strong taste of how the law went about digesting *causes célèbres*. Here was a case based on an incident – Neil Hamilton's alleged acceptance of Mohamed Fayed's brown envelopes – which had taken place in a few seconds. The case was covered in a page of court reporting in the newspapers on every day it came to court. Each page was jam-packed with the most relevant and titillating facts of the trial. The journalists and newspaper readers had a high old time feasting on the juiciest bits of the case.

Law doesn't allow lawyers to do that same cherry-picking of the highlights of a case. In *Hamilton v Fayed*, two barristers and four solicitors on each side took six months – and two large 18th-century drawing-roomfuls of files each, as I saw back in chambers – to prepare the case. Few sins remain interesting when their juice is stained across a thousand sheets of paper.

At least, though, in the end, those barristers and solicitors ended up with a judgment and their pictures on the front of the papers as they accompanied the winner or the loser out of the High Court. A few years later, when I did my pupillage, I was still keen to see one of these big-name judgments. I scanned the newspapers closely for big libel cases every day in the hope that I could sit in on at least one of them. No chance. There wasn't a single high-profile libel judgment in the whole year of my pupillage, anywhere in legal London. So I never got to see the moment of drama that marks the tensest moment of the case, the moment that no big legal-thriller film can do without, the moment when the foreman announces a verdict.

And it wasn't that I was unlucky, just that very few cases ever get that far because even the crossest and most self-assured plaintiff starts to get scared of losing. "The one great principle of the English law is to make business for itself," Dickens wrote in *Bleak House*. That's still true; it's just that those annoying bit-part players in the case, the clients, can throw a spanner in the works, particularly when they see how much good money they're throwing after bad.

Libel cases being so expensive – principally because the lawyers are so well-paid – they are particularly prone to settlement. The prospect of a case turning out like the one in *Bleak House* – "Jarndyce and Jarndyce still drags its dreary length before the Court, perennially hopeless" – fills all lawyers with excitement, but they rarely happen, unless one of the parties has exceptionally deep pockets or is willing to represent themselves.

That's why the McLibel case, which took two and a half years, was the longest in legal history: McDonald's, with bottomless pits of funds, could afford to take on a pair of penniless environ-mentalists prepared to represent themselves and defend their six-page factsheet, "What's Wrong with McDonald's", accusing the company of unhealthy practices in their food preparation.

I occasionally dropped in on the case – what the *Daily Telegraph* called "the best free entertainment in London". It was exactly that – for about ten minutes, as the two environmentalists, a gardener called Helen Steel and a postman called Dave Morris, laid into the company's alleged promotion of junk food, exploitation of workers and animals, advertising to children, and damage to the environment.

McDonald's argued back effectively and won the case, even if it was occasionally put on the back foot. At one point, its senior vice-president of marketing, David Green, admitted that, when he said McDonald's food was nutritious, and that it "provides nutrients and can be a part of a healthy balanced diet", the same could be said of sweets. Coca-Cola, too, was, he said, "nutritious" and was "providing water, and I think that is part of a balanced diet".

This is all good, knockabout stuff, but not for two and a half years, and certainly not if you're paying for it. Somewhere along the line, most clients, except for the really rich ones like McDonald's, start to worry about how the money they are trying to get off their opponents is being funnelled into the lawyers' pockets, and they decide to settle.

As a result, very few libel barristers ever get to see foremen read out verdicts more than a couple of times a year. The majority of barristers – with the exception of those doing criminal and family work, which rarely allow for great speeches – spend most of their time in their rooms going through files and preparing pleadings for cases which are usually settled out of court. A barrister may wait 15 or 20 years to become the lead protagonist in a big trial.

***

Even when barristers do get that sort of job, their hopes are often dashed at the last moment: one of Silas's later pupilmasters had a few years earlier been lined up to be part of the team representing Jonathan Aitken in his libel case against the *Guardian*. The paper had accused Aitken of staying in the Paris Ritz at the expense of an Arab associate, in contravention of ministerial rules.

When Silas arrived to work for the barrister on the case, the shelves that lined three sides of his large room and stretched from the floor to the ceiling where they worked were still filled up with a year's worth of files marked Aitken, a long time after the case had finished. The barrister had had conferences with his client, with witnesses, with his own solicitors, and with those of the other side, and he had been to court several times already to establish what evidence was eligible to be heard.

And, all the while, some heroic researcher had been carrying out the sort of task that is the classic stuff which cases are made up of, deeply dull and yet absolutely crucial; she had to go through all the bookings for the British Airways flights from Geneva to see if Aitken's wife, Lolicia, had been the one staying in the Ritz in Paris, as her husband was claiming.

So, on different sides of Europe, two people, Silas's pupilmaster and this researcher, were charged with long and dreary work, and all for a brief moment of triumph at the end: for Silas's pupilmaster, his day in court in defence of Aitken; for the researcher, Aitken's destruction. They couldn't both win.

In the end, it was Silas's pupilmaster who was the frustrated one. After weeks rummaging through a warehouse full of credit-card receipts, the researcher found the bookings slip showing that Lolicia Aitken and her children had been in the Geneva hotel for all the time that she was supposed to have been in Paris, contrary to what her husband had maintained.

Not only do most cases never come to a jury decision, because the great majority of them are settled out of court or, like the Aitken case, they collapse, but also, if your pupilmaster does happen to be involved in one that goes all the way, he will not be the one doing all the courtroom histrionics – the slapping of desks and the reducing of witnesses to tears.

He is necessarily the junior partner – known as the junior – to a QC, who does all the cross-examination. And QCs are too senior to take pupils. So, most of the time, given that you will be working on a case that never comes to trial, the pupil is the bridesmaid to the bridesmaid to a bride that never gets married. And, if the pupil is lucky enough to witness a marriage, the words used in the wedding ceremony are rarely inspiring. The language of the law – necessarily spare and bloodless to encapsulate hard, general principles – at the same time delights in a preference for the complicated over the simple: why say "depends on" when you happen to know that "predicated on" will do just as well? Lawyers always go for the complicated word even though they know, or perhaps because they know, that they are famous for over-elaboration. Dickens pointed out the tendency in *Bleak House*: " 'Not to put too fine a point upon it' – a favourite apology for plain-speaking with Mr Snagsby."

Sometimes, in an attempt to oversimplify, solicitors would go for simple words; but only where none would have been better. They liked pointless summaries at the end of covering notes for legal documents, something like: "That's basically where I am at the present time"; or "I suppose in simple terms where we sit now is saying, please go ahead."

***

However dreary it got, I couldn't countenance giving it all up. At a party just before I started as a pupil, I met a leading magazine executive, who had begun life as a journalist.

"Are you glad you made the change?" I asked.

"Oh yes. I wish I'd done it much earlier."

"Did you hate being a journalist?"

"No. It was absolutely wonderful. I just knew it was never going to be well-paid enough. And so I made the change. But far too late. All the really successful people I know started doing what they're doing as soon as they left university. They never had any hiccups and they never changed jobs. And they never wasted time on anything other than what they were supposed to be doing."

"How old were you when you changed?"

"23."

The conversation had a lasting effect on me, given that I had had several career changes between leaving university and taking up my law studies six years later – and I was now 31. Perhaps David Frobisher had been right never to see a film or read a book or laugh at a joke. After all, those sorts of things could all be done by lots of other people with none of the qualifications that I had. There are plenty of people who've seen lots of films and read lots of books; there are only so many successful and much-admired barristers.

Now, after these abortive career starts, I had convinced myself that jobs were not supposed to be enjoyable and this one just had to work. I was increasingly worried about what would happen if it didn't.

For the first few slip-ups in the careers I had chosen and failed in, I thought it was just a case of being in the wrong job. It takes time for those problems that others will define your life by – "Mark's a drunk" or "Jason has had loads of affairs" – to emerge. My own problem was now beginning to emerge: I had started a new job in a completely different field every autumn in the first three years after I had left university – as a literary journalist, a banker, an architectural historian – and now, several years further on, as a lawyer. With every job turning out to be the wrong job, I could see the horror of a pattern developing: that it might not be particular jobs that I disliked, just jobs full stop.

So I started looking for possibilities in anything and everything. I remember closely studying a photograph in the newspaper: "National Heritage Secretary, Peter Brooke, tightens the bolt of the metal corona on top of the newly-refurbished St Pancras Hotel in King's Cross, London" read the caption. The picture set me thinking – "Perhaps I should be a politician if quite a lot of it involves straightforward things like tightening up bolts and being photographed. Just the sort of thing I could do; I might even quite enjoy it."

Time seemed to be running out before I reached the stage where I would be considered a permanent dead loss. The wonderful blank canvas of youth – you could still become a professional footballer or the world's greatest novelist or anything, as long as you were still young enough for patterns of disaster, or lack of athleticism or intellectual gifts, not to have got in the way – was developing a great stain that spelt out the word, "failure".

I was feeling the march of time stamp out its physical effects as well. Just before I started pupil-lage, I was on the lavatory one morning, leaning forward and reading a book, when I felt something warm on my knee – my stomach. Soon after, lying in the bath, I noticed my stomach now crested the surface of the water while my chest followed a path parallel to the surface and just below it.

What's more my contemporaries were creeping ahead in their careers. They seemed so confident that they were doing the right job and would do it for life.

"There are only three jobs," said a friend's brother at a party when I was unemployed, just before I started my legal training.

"Oh, what are they?"

"Law, accountancy and banking."

"Which one do you do?"

"I was a solicitor. Now I'm a banker," he said, "And what do you do?"

It is at once the question the unemployed ask themselves more than any other and the one they dread being asked more than any other, the one that they try to manhandle conversations to avoid.

"Harry never does anything," said a nearby friend, chuckling.

At the time, I was so obsessed with my lack of a job that I made sure I wore a smart suit when I went out for the evening. I wore it one Saturday evening at a party at someone's parents' house in Kensington. Rich as the parents were, and successful as their daughter, an accountant, was, the party was being done on the cheap. The guests, dressed up in dressed-down clothes, smoked ropy joints in a circle round a big salad bowl full of fruit punch on a large kitchen table. As each guest turned up, they emptied whatever bottle of spirits they had into the bowl.

As I poured my bottle of gin in, carefully and at a distance so as not to splash my one good suit, an old schoolfriend, who had gone straight into the law on leaving university, accosted me.

"Hi, Harry. How are you?"

"Very well, thanks."

"Still unemployed?"

"How can you tell?"

"No one with a job wants to wear a suit at the weekend."

Even in compliments I could find insults. At a pub quiz one evening, an actor friend and I got the lion's share of the answers right.

"God, you're lucky," said another member of the team, a journalist.

"Why?"

"Because you don't have an office job, you can spend your time reading good things and learning useful stuff. I spend my whole life doing really dreary office administration with only about five minutes every day of actual writing."

He was genuinely trying to compliment us, but all I could do was envy his life, a life where he was forced by a boss to do something, however dull; as against my free life at the time, where I could do – or read – anything I wanted, but more often than not wasted my days with a bit of newspaper-reading, eked out with domestic tasks.

Why was I so different from my contemporaries? Practically all of them had settled into jobs within months of leaving university and were still doing them five years on. And, for that matter, why was I so different to the other people in my chambers? To an outsider, we would have all looked alike.

We were all stuffed full of the same exams, had often done the same subjects and been to the same universities, even the same schools. They got on with it perfectly happily. I didn't.

The whole set-up would have been even more unbearable if I hadn't benefited, not so much from wearing exactly the same old school tie as the other barristers in chambers, but from having been to the same sort of schools that gave the same sort of education.

At the end of my first day of pupillage, there was a party to celebrate the appointment of a member of chambers as a High Court judge. I went with Silas.

We talked to each other for most of the evening but, after about an hour, Julian Woodhouse, the rights of way expert, left the group he had been talking to and made his way over to us.

"We were just wondering," he asked, "if either of you could remember the words Virgil uses to describe how Neptune calms the storm in Book One of the *Aeneid*. Denning referred to it once in a great judgment of his."

"Oh yes, I know the bit," I said, remembering my O-level Latin, "It's where Aeneas has almost died in the same storm. On his way to found Rome."

"Yes, that's right," Julian said. "Can you remember the quote?"

"No. I'm afraid not. But I do remember the later one, when they're shipwrecked and he's trying to comfort Achates. *'Forsan et haec olim meminisse etiam iuvabit'* – 'One day, it will be a pleasure to remember even these horrible things.'"

"Yes. That wasn't the quote I meant."

Julian moved back to the other side of the room.

"It's all right for you then, isn't it?" Silas said. "You're right in there."

"I didn't remember the quote, though."

"Well, you still managed to.... " Silas paused for effect, "get some fucking Latin in, didn't you, you absolute cunt?"

Silas was right about my tactics. He hadn't been taught Latin and, during the discussion about Virgil, I had done nothing to include him; quite the opposite, in fact. I had feverishly curried favour with Julian, with a hidden delight that Silas had been left in the lurch.

Silas was wrong, though, when he said it was all right for me. Knowing Latin and coming from the same world as all these people was not enough to make me enjoy the job. But, with my mounting total of career mistakes, I couldn't now give up, or turn to friends and family for consolation. They would have been sympathetic, I know, but they couldn't have actually made the job any more enjoyable – any more than knowing a bit of Virgil might have.

Bored and miserable by my activities during the day, I was desperate not to waste my evenings. At the weekend, when my tiredness at the week's tensions took over, I was perfectly happy going to bed at 11 or 12, even though I was free to wake up at whatever time I wanted. In the week, however, when I had to be up at 7.30, I put off bedtime until the small hours and tried to pack in as much into the evening as possible. I either got determinedly drunk with friends on a serious mission to enjoy myself, or read highbrow books, depressed by the dreariness of the things I had to read at work.

**

I read literature about the law in search of consolation. But, because of the romanticisation of the subject, I found none of the sympathy that novels and poems usually bring, none of the reassurance that others have felt as miserable doing the same thing. Stephen Fry has written of the relief in his youth of coming across Oscar Wilde and other gay authors and realising that his condition was not unique.

As it became more and more likely that I would never get a tenancy and would have to settle for some less illustrious job, I found it easy to dig up plenty of people and books who could give me some consolation: they proved, say, that material wealth mattered for little and that a high-paid job wasn't the be-all and end-all. But I couldn't find any books to cheer me up in the state I was then in, books that might relieve the misery of imprisonment in the corner of a lawyer's room researching land disputes – it was hardly Dickens's blacking factory.

So I began to construct my own elaborate consolations for my 'condition', as I saw it. The fact that being a barrister was considered an impressive job made a difference. Although I was living like a prisoner on evening release, kept in a room for nine hours a day – and although I felt like a prisoner – it was not the same as actually being a prisoner. Most people, brought up on books and television programmes full of rich and dashing barristers, thought I was in a good and interesting job. I saw no reason to tell them otherwise; I didn't want every conversation turning into an exchange of complaints on my part and pity on the other.

Days grew so similar to each other that I could be cheered up by the tiniest of differences: a slightly quicker journey home from work, a goodish book at lunchtime. I hoovered up poetry and prose that I hadn't bothered with before because it was too difficult: *Anna Karenina*, which I'd tried before and found impossible, slipped down easily and painlessly, and I learnt chunks of Keats and Shelley to recite in my head at low moments in court.

Still, I never managed to persuade myself that, as long as the mind is free to roam, that's all that matters. I couldn't be like Hitler's architect, Albert Speer, who in his daily walks round Spandau Prison in Berlin, could convince himself in his mind's eye that he was actually walking through the Alps near his old holiday chalet, or round Venice or Rio or other great cities he had visited when he was free, or read about in his cell.

I did, though, in a sort of Speer-like way, try to squeeze as much pleasure as I could out of the day. I angled my chair to get a sideways glance of the view from the window when David was out of the room, but only moving it a little out of position. That way, I didn't have to do too much obvious re-positioning when he came back in.

From this vantage point I could see a wall, a roof, some scaffolding, a bit of the law courts and some sky. And I stared at these with an intensity that I had never before applied to ordinary objects. I could look at them for whole minutes at a time, until I heard the familiar footfall outside the room and the turn of the doorknob.

Once, when I was staring at the roof of the building opposite that Don the builder used to waddle across, it started to rain. I picked out one grey slate in particular and concentrated on it. First it was spotted with silver raindrops which, once there were enough of them, took on the look of a web of snail's trails. Once the drops had covered the surface of the tile, the grey colour of the slate changed to an opaque white.

I wondered how the eye could recognise the same object as being a slate, not only in these three disguises – grey, covered in snail's trails, and white – but also in the countless others that would come with sleet or sunshine or mizzle.

One summer afternoon, I stared for some time at the way light shimmered on the motes in the bowl of a loo in Gray's Inn. And, every morning in the spring I got a little lift in my spirits from the seagull that screamed from its nest on the chimney stack of Inner Temple library.

Other springs of consolation – tiny ones – dripped out of unusual places. In the humourless world of the law, little jokes became much funnier. I liked the private detective who cropped up in one case – Roger Mann Esq, Finlays Bureau of Investigation Ltd (FBI), Norwood North. Or a Californian judgment by an American Indian judge – "an early decision by Judge Learned Hand".

Dry legal documents sometimes got so dry that they suddenly became amusing. In a long trial in Oxfordshire over a building dispute, I recorded and transcribed whole conversations between a Henley solicitor and his client.

"We'll short-circuit it, if we can, to move it forward. You're going to provide information – then it's back to Great Milton and fire up the photocopier."

This same solicitor scooped the prize for the greatest sentence I saw in my year as a pupil – "I don't really like to use the word globalisation because our business depends on local application and service; it doesn't matter how large the world is. I prefer to say global localisation and gain economies by allocating lead responsibilities."

At the time, I copied down a passage from *Anna Karenina*: "There are no conditions of life to which a man cannot accustom himself, especially if he sees that every one around him lives in the same way."

I felt this particularly keenly when I compared notes with Silas.

One lunchtime, he knocked gingerly on my door.

"Come in."

Silas was pale and tight-lipped. Once he'd seen that David wasn't in the room, he pulled his chair over towards mine.

"Has David left for lunch?"

"Yes. What's wrong?"

His face relaxed for a moment.

"Alec has really gone too far. This morning... this morning, he... "

Silas took several deep breaths and tried to speak but couldn't, without his voice breaking. He raised his eyes to the ceiling.

"I'm sorry."

"Don't be sorry. Cry if you want."

He didn't say anything for a while. I went and got him a glass of water. By the time I got back, he'd composed himself.

"When I came in this morning, Alec asked me to come over to his desk and help him with something."

"What about the exclusion zone?"

"Well, exactly. I thought something quite good

must be about to happen if he was prepared to let me come within a yard of him.

"I'd just got inside the exclusion zone, when he said, 'Stop. Stand there and don't move.' "

"Oh come on, Silas. I'm sorry to sound harsh, but you can't get too upset. You've known about the exclusion zone for months."

"Yes, but that wasn't it this time. He's never got me to stand on the edge of the zone before. I asked him what he wanted me to do and he just said, 'Stand there. No, just a little bit to your right. Forward a bit. There. That's perfect. Now, just move a little to your left every minute or so – parallel to the window frame – whenever I say "left".'

"Well, that doesn't sound too bad. What did he do next?"

"Nothing. Just kept me moving bit by bit. He was making me into a sunshade for his computer screen. For the whole morning, I've been a fucking sundial, slowly moving round the room."

He choked these last words out and, for the first time, cried a little.

"Oh God, Silas. That is terrible," I said. Whenever I heard his horror stories before, I felt a little relief – the worse they were, the better my chances of tenancy. I hardly felt that at all this time.

"You must complain. You can't go back in there this afternoon."

"No, I can't complain. You know I can't. Anyway, the afternoon won't be so bad."

"Why not?"

"His room is east-facing."

**

It is wrong to make out that the Bar is brimful of evil. There were some decent people around the Inns of Court, who if anything showed up the indecency of the rest of them.

The woman barrister in David Frobisher's chambers, Sara Cartwright, had all the good manners and delivered all the pleasantries I was used to in the outside world.

"You're Harry Mount, aren't you?" she said to me as we both walked towards Julian Woodhouse's room for tea. "I'm Sara Cartwright. I live upstairs in the attic."

"Oh, how do you do?" I said. I was a little shocked. We weren't actually talking in the tea room – we were standing in the corridor outside, while Alec, Silas and David filed past towards Julian's room, all flicking a surprised sideways glance at Sara. All the same, Sara's approach was highly unorthodox because: a) barristers didn't introduce themselves to pupils – even now, two months after I had started pupillage, I had talked to only seven of the 20 barristers in chambers, and I only knew the names of the other 13, including Sara, because I had a small client's guide to chambers with pictures of all the members in it; b) barristers didn't even talk to each other in corridors for fear of setting the precedent of striking up conversation every time they bumped into a colleague in the building; c) she STUCK OUT HER HAND.

"Oh God, you don't do all that refusing to shake hands stuff, do you?"

"I thought it was a rule."

"It is," she said, leaning forward to whisper in my ear, "But do you know what happens if you break rules like that?"

"No," I whispered back.

"Absolutely bugger all," she said, raising her voice.

Three faces – Alec's, Silas's, and David's – whipped round in our direction and then whipped back in the direction they had been looking, into their teacups.

"Who's your pupilmaster?" she said.

"David Frobisher," I said quietly, so he couldn't hear.

"Oh right." She paused, raising her eyebrows. "He's working on an adverse possession case, isn't he? Does that mean you are too?"

"Yes."

"Has he shown you McDonnell on Adverse Possession?"

"No."

"Oh. It really is crucial. I couldn't have survived pupillage without it. David really should have."

***

Sara broke off mid-sentence. She was very nearly angry with David, but that would have been a breach of *omertà* – fellow barrister first, pupil second. "If he hasn't got a copy, do come up and borrow mine. I'm the last shoebox on the right."

"What were you talking to Sara for?" said David when I walked into the room.

"She said I should read McDonnell on Adverse Possession."

"Won't be much help."

"Not to worry. She said I could borrow hers."

"Here. I've got a spare."

David threw the slim blue hardback he was reading towards me, flicking it through the air like a hard-driven Frisbee.

"Thanks."

I had no phone on my desk and so had to risk using David's when he went to the lavatory.

"Hello, Sara. It's Harry Mount. Just to say – David's lending me Adverse Possession."

"Had a copy in easy reach, did he?"

"Erm... I'm not sure. Anyway, I won't be needing yours. Many thanks."

"OK. Fine," Sara said, with a friendly laugh laid over the top of the comment. That friendly laugh stuck in my mind. Any of the other barristers might have said exactly those same words, but they wouldn't have bothered with the extra effort of the little laugh on top.

**

I found little pockets of gentility elsewhere in the Inns of Court. The most surprising acts of kindness came from an unusual quarter: the man who had been my chief reason for going to the Bar, not because of his kindness, but because of his brilliance – George Carman.

Towards the end of my pupillage, just before the decisions over who would get tenancy were made, I got the chance to work with him.

"We're in court this morning," said my last pupil-master, Darius Glover, as I came through the door.

"Oh good."

"Yup, we're meeting George in half an hour, so you'd better get ready."

I didn't ask who George was – that sort of follow-up conversation wasn't encouraged. But I got a fairly good idea who he was from the way Darius dropped the name without the surname.

We made the short walk through the Temple in silence. As we crossed the road, I saw a familiar-looking diminutive figure, swamped by solicitors, standing outside the Royal Courts of Justice – the great white Gothic fortress that divides the Strand from Fleet Street, and Westminster from the City of London.

"Hello, George," said Darius.

"Oh hello, Darius. Who's this with you?"

"My pupil."

"Has he got a name?"

Darius introduced me.

"How do you do?" said George.

He didn't shake my hand, but he put a lot of enthusiasm into the greeting.

"We're in court in a moment, George," said the senior solicitor in the group that huddled around him as they queued up to have their belongings X-rayed before going into the High Court. "Here are the prosecution bundles. Here's the relevant case law. Do you need anything else?"

"20 Silk Cut."

A solicitor in his late 40s was sent to a news-agent's on Fleet Street, and the rest of us marched into court.

After a morning spent discussing a procedural point in an unnewsworthy case, Carman took me and Darius to lunch in the Royal Courts of Justice café. The normal form for me would have been to keep quiet and draw legal lessons from their conversation as they discussed their holidays.

"How are you enjoying being a pupil?" said Carman, as soon as we sat down.

"It's very enjoyable and useful," I said.

"Really? That seems an odd thing to say. It's always struck me as a disastrous way of learning things."

"Well, yes, it has its faults," I said, glancing in Darius's direction. "But I don't see how it can be improved on."

"Not being closeted in a room for eight hours a day with someone 20 years older than you, might be a start. Wouldn't it, Darius?"

"I'm sure you're right, George," said Darius with a grim smile.

"Anyway, what do you think of the case?"

"I think we've got a good chance, George," said Darius.

"Not you," said Carman, "What do you think, Harry?"

"I think we've got a good chance."

"Quite right. Spot on."

In court that day, Carman had little to do. When the case came to trial a few weeks later, though, it transpired that he won. My happy encounter with him made me all the more admiring of the time I'd seen him in full flow a few years earlier, representing

Mohamed Fayed against Neil Hamilton.

Like all my experiences of big cases, this was not the trial proper – that was to be Carman's last case, and was held a few months later – and he was there only to argue a complex procedural point.

Carman's argument was that, since the Nolan Committee on Parliamentary Standards had already decided that Hamilton had behaved improperly, it would be a wrongful interference with the supremacy of Parliament for a court to quash a parliamentary decision by siding with Hamilton.

It was a tenuous argument – it was later held that the decision of the Nolan Committee was not on a level with a parliamentary decision, ie, Hamilton could still contest the case. So, with the odds stacked against him, Carman did not have much of a chance to shine on the afternoon I watched him in action. But that didn't stop his legal team swooping down on him, making clucking, admiring noises at every break in the proceedings.

"Well done, George," said one of the senior solicitors.

"What about the case; when will it get to trial?" said the other senior solicitor.

"No idea."

"What are our chances?" said Darius.

"No idea."

"Got the Nolan point across beautifully," said the solicitor in his late 40s. "What next?"

"20 Silk Cut," Carman said, holding back the barrage of inquiries with the same deep, even tones that he used in court. There was no trace of his native Lancashire in his voice but his English – which, though certainly received, was not as fruity as his 70-year-old public-school-educated contemporaries – retained a gentle lilt that might have owed something to his Blackpool youth.

His personal charm was so great, and his gravitas in court so convincing, that I rather came round to the side of his client, Mohamed Fayed, who I had had no sympathy with in the past.

The other point in Fayed's favour was fairly overpowering – he won. Victory in the libel courts is a fairly good sign of innocence. As Geoffrey Robertson, the leading libel QC, has written, "London is the libel capital of the world. No other legal system offers such advantages to the wealthy maligned celebrity: procedures that tilt the odds in favour of plaintiffs; a law that gives little weight to the principles of freedom of expression; and tax-free damages awarded unrestrainedly by star-struck juries who dislike newspapers."

Neil Hamilton may not have been rich but, with financial help from others, he had got together a star legal team. And still, despite being the plaintiff and having all the advantages that Geoffrey Robertson points out, he lost.

It didn't help his case that he and his wife were so unprepossessing. Neil Hamilton sat at the front of court next to his solicitor while Christine Hamilton sat further back, where the pupils of all the barristers in the case and I were sitting. Every time a point was made in the Hamiltons' favour by their lawyer – which was, after all, the lawyer's job, irrespective of whether the points were true or not – Neil Hamilton turned round and gave his wife a drippy smile, as if the case had been clinched that very moment.

There was a mixture of comfortable padded seats and hard, wooden ones at the back of the modern court, which was in an annexe to the main Victorian building of the Royal Courts. The comfortable ones always went first and, as one of the first into court in the morning, I usually got one of them.

On the morning that turned me against Christine Hamilton, I got the last comfy seat, just next to the point where the hard seats began. Christine Hamilton came in late and filed past me to a hard seat. A few hours later, I nipped out to the lavatory.

It was clear I was not leaving court – I had been there for the previous week, sitting in the comfortable seats for the full court session every day. But, when I returned, Christine Hamilton had stolen my seat. So I had to file past her to the wooden seats. She didn't say a word as I settled down next to her, but just gazed fixedly ahead at her husband, awaiting the wet smile.

That sort of selfishness was not unusual among libel litigants. You could see why someone has to go to court when they commit a crime, and why personal fallings-out mean divorces between perfectly amenable people might have to end up in court. But to sue for libel essentially means going to court over your reputation – the test of whether or not something is libellous depends on whether a statement is likely to make reasonable and respectable people think less of the plaintiff. And the sort of people who go to court over their reputation are usually in possession of an oversized ego.

"Never go to law," was one of David's catchphrases, if you could call something he said on two occasions over the course of three months a catchphrase. He may have been an angry egomaniac – and angry egomaniacs like litigation – but he was a barrister, and barristers don't like litigation when it involves them personally.

"We know how much we like to charge – and we know we're terrible value for money," said Sara Cartwright outside tea in one of our illicit conversations. "It's the same with divorce lawyers. They never get divorced."

It sounded more convincing from Sara than from Silas whose source for the same observation had been Alec McArdle.

"Even if they hate each other?"

"Especially if they hate each other. That's when people really forget how much we cost."

"If you know it's right, then, not to go to court for a divorce and certainly not for libel," I said, settling into the door-frame of the stationery cupboard, keeping my voice low, because David was at that very moment passing by, on his way back from tea, and might have overheard me enjoying a conversation, "you'll always be representing idiots or bastards, won't you?"

"Yeees," said Sara, like a *Playschool* presenter.

"Isn't that pretty miserable?"

"There's no legal aid for libel."

"So?"

"Well, you must have known that you were never going to be defending the downtrodden masses. If you end up doing libel, you'll be defending Robert Maxwells because," Sara said, pronouncing each word separately and deliberately, "Robert... Maxwells... can... afford... to... pay."

Maxwell had discovered early in his career that the threat of a libel writ is an effective block to newspapers publishing the truth. I now know this from the other side, as a journalist. Whenever someone instructs lawyers over a libel that has been committed or is in danger of being committed, a piece of paper goes round a newspaper office with a warning to be careful about the injured party.

Journalists, who want to keep their jobs, are, contrary to type, careful to tell the truth, when getting it wrong could mean the paper – or, if they're freelance, the journalists themselves – losing large sums of money. As Aneurin Bevan said, when greater state censorship of the press was mooted, there is "no need to muzzle sheep".

Sara told me a lot along these lines. She was particularly good on Carman, who she had known well. Carman was keen on women. One, Karen Maxfield, 30 years his junior, had been his constant companion in his last years, and was left a considerable amount of money on his death. Sara, in her mid-40s and unmarried, was still attractive. George confided in her, without, it seems, offending Karen Maxfield, who was not in a sexual relationship with him.

"He was very kind to me when I met him," I told Sara, when we bumped into each other in a Fleet Street bar towards the end of my pupillage.

"He would be," she said. "He had a terrible start himself."

Sara went on to tell me how, at the beginning of his career, aged 25, he had contracted an ill-fated marriage with a market researcher on whose earnings, his wife claimed, he depended to subsidise his paltry income as a lowly criminal hack. Carman does not include his first wife in his *Who's Who* entry.

"I saw her once," said Sara. "She came to court to confront him. I didn't know who she was at the time and, when she left, I asked George who she was.

"He said, 'That was my first wife,' and never mentioned her again."

The first Mrs Carman has given her own account of the reunion.

"George swept past me, saying to a colleague, 'Oh, there's that woman I told you about.' It hurt me to the quick. For, while he was unknown and struggling, 'that woman' worked in a canteen to keep food on our table."

His first disastrous marriage was followed by another two.

"That's why you only ever see him with other barristers – no family life," Sara told me. "Meets them in Daly's in the Strand after work, buys them lots of champagne, goes to a restaurant and then tries to take them home."

"And did he ever... meet you in Daly's?"

Our corridor meetings – half-public, half-private, frowned upon by everybody else – had a sort of confessional nature, keenly set on edge by the teatime purdah we were always about to undergo or had just been through.

"I got as far as the restaurant."

"Bit of a sad way to pass old age?"

"Yes," Sara said. "Either that... or a very good way."

***

Whether the personal side of his life was sad or not, Carman had certainly cracked the professional side so beautifully that he avoided all the bits of the job I hated – the years spent in your room filling files with paper, then putting them on your shelves, then taking them down and then re-reading them.

Ever since he first made his mark, defending Jeremy Thorpe in 1979, Carman's fine oratory meant he was reserved by chambers expressly for court appearances. So other barristers did most of the dreary paperwork while he was brought in for the denouement – the exciting bit of the case.

Like F. E. Smith and Rumpole of the Bailey, he stood for a type that is rare in real life – the master of the beautifully weighted, erudite phrase – but has stuck tenaciously in people's minds as the exemplar of the barrister. When an opportunity for a great speech did present itself, few of the barristers had the sort of broad intelligence to rise to the occasion. Brilliant as some of their minds are, those minds are best suited to plotting a course through mountains of facts and picking out a neat, straight line towards success. Anything that speaks of originality or lateral thinking or non-legal reading is rare.

And anything resembling a good joke was likely to be frowned on. Professor Edward Burn of Christ Church, Oxford, the leading land law expert in the country, and a war hero, gave entertaining occasional lectures which I attended as part of my legal training.

"Don't expect to enjoy reading your textbooks," he said in an introductory lecture. "I've just got the proofs of the latest edition of my book on land law. The publishers were very polite. They were delighted with the manuscript, they said, but they had had a problem with one of the cases I cited." Professor Burn's hawkish, normally enthusiastic face drooped. "They hadn't been able to find any reference in any other books anywhere to one Chancery case I referred to. The case was called

Jarndyce v Jarndyce. Could I help them find it?"

Other barristers could get carried away by their own eloquence. And they certainly were eloquent. Years of speaking in public had blasted away any lingering nerves and they could talk on any subject without notes or hesitation or repetition. Still, it didn't mean they were particularly good at speaking. In fact, not feeling any fear was a bad thing: fear meant that you kept your speeches short and practised them often, particularly if you were making "amusing" speeches. At the end of the party where Julian Woodhouse had talked Latin with me, the host, who was giving the party to celebrate being made a High Court judge, made a speech. It was based on the premise that he was dictating his words on to a voice-recognition recorder which would then type out what it had heard: "My gourds, ladles and gentlemen," he opened confidently.

At their best, the sharpest barristers could be impressive speakers and arguers. On the day that Lord Denning died, all the judges in the Court of Appeal, where I was sitting in on a case for the morning, gathered in court behind Lord Woolf, the Master of the Rolls, while he paid an apparently impromptu tribute to Denning. Without a stumble or a pause – or notes – he gave a moving and simple speech: an adroit mix of personal reminiscences and a two-minute-long précis of a legal career that had lasted almost 60 years.

But even Lord Woolf paled into insignificance next to Carman. By the time of *Hamilton v Fayed*, Carman was almost 70, and had only two years to live, but he was still at the height of his powers. I was no longer a pupil or a mini-pupil, so I had no insider's way into getting a seat in court. Still, I managed to get into the public gallery for the final day of the case.

Everything was much as I had left it a year earlier: the same courtroom, the same waves and waves of solicitors and lawyers; Christine Hamilton was still in the comfortable seats.

With an extremely relaxed manner, Carman dealt with the new arguments that were consistently thrown up by his opponent with exactly the right answer, combining lightning-quick thinking and a large amount of facts trawled from the months of research that had gone into the build-up of the trial. With his quiverful of forensic skills – and Neil

Hamilton's pattern of admitting only the sins that had been proved against him and vigorously denying anything else – victory looked secure as soon as the jury left the room.

**

At the time that Carman was winning the case for Mohamed Fayed, the next stage after pupillage beckoned. I debated whether to apply for tenancy. If I was going to, the accepted practice was to go for both the chambers I had done pupillage in – the annexe ran a separate tenancy scheme from the main building   and in several others.

"You might as well," said Sara.

"Why?" I said, more loudly than usual. Although David was no longer my pupilmaster, and I only ever saw him at tea, the thought of him overhearing me was still enough to bring on the fear of a small lecture on the perils of talking out of turn. He was in the next-door room, where I knew he could hear me, but I was demob happy, now that I was no longer a pupil. I might come back but, if I did, it would be as a tenant, where I could talk as loudly as I wanted, whether I was slouching imperiously in the door-frame of the stationery cupboard, or slowly sipping my tea, catching people's eyes and looking, not down into my cup, but wherever I wanted – out of the window, up at the ceiling, in people's faces even.

"Well, you've got nothing else to do."

"A powerful point – but not one that's stopped me giving up jobs in the past."

"Yup. But that's when you were young, when you could say, 'I'm unemployed!'" Sara said with a burst of enthusiasm, finishing the sentence on a high note. "Now you'll have to say," – she dropped a semitone – 'I'm unemployed.'"

"I still am quite young, aren't I?"

"Yes, but not young enough. You're old enough to do what we all do – go on doing something boring because you've worked out there isn't anything better to do."

"Is that it?"

"That – and the very important fact that you'll keep your parents happy. I'm 43 and I still wouldn't give up my job – I couldn't bear to tell my mother."

I went back to my first chambers, the only one of the two where I had done my pupillages that had a vacancy. There I was to take a test with the other applicants. What had amounted to the longest job interview in the world – six months spent in the building with my prospective new employers, and another six months with their colleagues – apparently wasn't enough to determine whether I was good enough to be taken on.

It had been several months since I had last seen David. I bumped into him in the ground-floor waiting room, on my way in to take my test. He was sitting on the sofa, reading a paper.

"Hello," I said.

"Hello," he said, with the usual wrench it took him to force a smile. Then he looked back down at the paper he had been reading.

"How are you?" I said.

"Fine," he replied, still looking at the paper.

"I'm taking the tenancy test. Upstairs, I think."

"Hmmm."

A little burst of the old rudeness was bearable, nostalgic even. Even if I got the tenancy, I would never have to spend as much time in the same room as him ever again. He would stay in his single drawing room. I would stay in mine. And, even if we were in adjoining single drawing rooms for ever, the two panelled Georgian doors that would separate us might as well have been two large cornfields – in our three months together, he had addressed as few words to the barrister in the next-door room as he had to me.

In the exam room, there was only one other candidate, Silas, and the invigilating barrister, Julian Woodhouse, whose room this was – the room where I had had tea every day for six months. Julian said nothing.

"Hello, Silas."

"Oh, hello," he said. He followed up his awkward smile with a hammed-up look of startled shock at the difficulty of the approaching test. I had expected him to be there but didn't know for sure – we hadn't talked much since I had moved on to the annexe, and he had stayed in the main building. Neither of us had revealed to the other that we were going for the same tenancy.

"Better start straight away," said Woodhouse.

The test involved a question about charitable trusts – a subject neither of us had done much of in the previous year.

"God, that was awful," Silas said, once it was over and we had got out on to Fleet Street, heading towards an awful Irish-themed pub, where we knew there wouldn't be any barristers.

"Yup. Absolutely impossible."

We both knew that the test had been difficult, but not that difficult. Still, we left it at that – agreeing to agree that it had been impossible, giving each of us a get-out clause if we didn't pull off the tenancy – and didn't talk any more about the test. For a year, on and off, the two of us had been engaged in two battles: first, to insist that we were each having a worse time than the other, second, to get a tenancy. We both knew that the first battle was a disingenuous one, the second the only one that mattered.

Although we used to talk openly about most things, there was no way we could talk frankly about either of the battles, although we were waging them day in, day out. Now, there was no point in taking either contest any further. There was nothing more we could do to influence the outcome before we got our letters with the chambers' decision.

So we contented ourselves with getting drunk on Caffrey's lager and concentrating on the frivolous aspects of the past year.

***

We are sorry to say that you have not been successful in your application for tenancy. We wish you the best of luck in your legal career.

I was upset but not shocked. I had prepared myself for this letter from the beginning of my legal education, when, in our introductory class, we had been told how unlikely it was that any of us would end up getting a tenancy.

What was more shocking was what happened to Silas. One of the things that had emerged about him over our year of pupillage was that he received his post earlier than me every day. Perhaps it had something to do with where he lived – near the Mount Pleasant sorting office, on the fringes of King's Cross and Islington. For whatever reason, now that I'd got my letter from chambers, he certainly would have got his.

Another more obvious fact about him was his self-deprecation. If he had been rejected, he would have been on the phone to me immediately. If he had been accepted, knowing there was only one vacancy, he could not have faced making the call –

he hated to crow. So, either his letter had got lost in the post or he had just secured a job for life.

"Hello."

"Hello, Silas. It's me. Has the letter arrived?"

"You?"

"Yup. Not good, I'm afraid."

"Oh God. I'm sorry."

"What about you?"

"Yes, the letter's arrived."

He knew what implications his success had for my career but he hadn't been able to state them openly. His good manners meant he had to ask me how I had done, even though he knew the answer. We ran through the right mixture of commiseration and congratulation, and promised to meet for a drink.

**

I wasn't taken on by any other chambers either. Why should they take on an unknown quantity when they already had several pupils, whose qualities and faults they knew inside out, all fighting for a place?

Once I discovered that there was to be a finite end to my legal career, I literally counted the hours until it would all be over: in the middle of August, I worked out on the back of an envelope that I had 517 hours of pupillage left.

"Lucky you," said Silas, when we met in the Irish-themed pub in Fleet Street again, "That's only about 20 days' worth... if you worked 24-hour days."

"Yup. But after that I've got to work out what to do in the tricky gap between giving up the Bar and retiring."

"Ah yes. What about a holiday? Italy will be lovely at the end of September."

"Excellent. That'll take me nicely up to the middle of October."

"Well, think of me then, sweating away on rights of access to hedges and ditches."

"You're right," I said, slipping into a serious tone after the third pint of Caffrey's. "But I would have liked to have at least been offered tenancy."

"Then you would have taken it," Silas said, "And been miserable."

"You're right. I'm too vain to turn it down, even though I know how much I'd hate it." I took a long sip of beer to compose a way of reversing the implied insult. "And it is an impressive thing to pull off."

"You don't really think that," said Silas. "There's no need to be kind."

"Lots of people do think that."

"Yes, but not you," said Silas, himself a little serious now. "Not that you should."

"The terrible thing is, that I do actually. I may have hated every minute but that doesn't mean that, if I had liked it, I would have walked off with a tenancy."

"That's good of you to say."

"It's not good. It's just the truth. The miserable thing is that it worked."

"What do you mean?"

"That the whole idea of pupillage worked – the horror of a whole year spent trying to get a job sorts out the ones that are really good from the ones that are just OK."

"I'm sure that's not true. You were just as... "

"Oh Silas, please stop being so self-deprecating."

"Well, I suppose I never minded it quite as much as you."

"Which means that you're better at it than me."

"No, it doesn't."

"Yes, it does. It means you spend more time doing

it and, when you are doing it, you spend more time thinking about it. And less time thinking about how much you hate it."

"Well, yes, I suppose so," said Silas. "But anyway, whoever's better – or whoever they think's better... "

"Silas!"

"OK. Whoever's better – they could just give them the job straight off, instead of forcing them through a year of hell."

"Yeees. But, in some cases," I said, pointing my finger at Silas, "talent takes some time to emerge."

"Fair enough. I was a bit quiet for the first week."

"First six months," I said. "And you haven't been to public school. Or Oxford. And you didn't know the Neptune passage from Book One of the *Aeneid*, you utter fool."

Silas was bound to turn out a good barrister. He had bounced me into justifying a system I hated and he had done so by using only politeness and self-deprecation.

"But still," I continued, "I don't see why they don't just call pupillage 'a job' and then give you – or rather me – the sack when you don't turn out to be as good as the quiet, weirdo, state-school boy who can't speak Latin."

"Oi tink you'll be about hitting the nail on the head," said Silas, adopting a bad Irish accent as he picked up our fourth round of Caffrey's from the bar.

***

I didn't punch the air when I walked out of chambers for the last time. Like a lot of things you do for the last time – the last time you see an old friend before you finally drift apart, the last time you're sick from drinking too much, the last time you go to a night-club – it only becomes clear that it was the last time a few months later.

When it came to the law, I only made the conscious decision to give it all up in the December after the September I left chambers. Until then, there was a chance I would end up in another chambers, or even in the chambers where I had done my pupillage, if a vacancy ever emerged. I was still able to convince myself that the best way to get over the horror was by sticking with the job until the raw pain dulled into everyday irritation.

The misery I had gone through only crystallised when I knew I wouldn't return; when I no longer had to condition myself to the idea that I might have to continue in that same world until retirement. The indignities I had been prepared to undergo only assumed their full, nightmarish shape in retrospect, when I ended up in a job – as a journalist – which I enjoyed in the company of more humane people, in a world where those indignities would have been ridiculed for being exactly that.

I had one final cold blast of the Bar the following February, a few months after I had decided to give it up for good. I was making a few preliminary steps to becoming a journalist but had not got beyond a few book reviews and the odd freelance article. It was the perfect time to don rose-tinted spectacles: far enough away from the acute misery of it all to start mythologising my time as a pupil; near enough that I could still change my mind and keep applying to chambers, even though every month I was away was a month for prospective employers to ask, "And why is it, Mr Mount, that you've taken so long to get your act together?"

The cold blast was heartening, a reminder of

what had really happened to make me so low throughout that horrible year.

***

During my pupillage, a pupil in a different chambers was in the process of taking her chambers to court because it had failed to pay her the minimum wage. Pupillages, as a form of apprenticeship, had originally been made exempt from the minimum-wage legislation. Her argument was that, far from being an apprenticeship, pupillage was proper work, with plenty of services carried out in exactly the same way that a fully-fledged barrister would have done them; services for which she could have charged much more than the minimum wage.

The case had been discussed in my chambers one summer afternoon, while it was going on just up the road at the High Court. When tea finished, Darius Glover cornered me in the corridor where Sara and I used to talk.

Sara walked out of the tea room just after Darius, saw him talking to me and struck a joke expression for my benefit – half exaggerated shock, half quizzical – before climbing to her attic room.

"You've heard about this minimum-wage case, have you?" Darius asked.

"Yes."

"And are you thinking of taking out an action against us?"

One of the few benefits – if it is a benefit – the law had taught me was never to give a concession without getting something in return.

"I must say I hadn't thought about it. But, now that you ask me, I might but I don't think I will. It wouldn't be very helpful for my chances of tenancy, would it?"

"It won't have any effect at all, I promise."

"Even so, it's not fair on chambers, really. When I accepted the pupillage, I knew I wasn't going to be paid anything at all."

"You know none of that matters if the law changes," said Darius, a little testy now. "If she wins, you win. So you might take out a case?"

"Yes, I might."

Some time after I ended my pupillage, the pupil's case came to court and she won, setting a legal precedent for all pupils. Still, I didn't think for a moment of taking out an action.

Then I was invited back to the Inner Temple to discuss the case. The head clerk, who had always been polite but dismissive when I had been a pupil, was friendly when he called up to suggest a time I might meet the barrister in chambers responsible for pupils. The barrister himself, Francis Garton, had undergone an even more extreme conversion. A dry, well-fed figure in his late 60s, he had barely acknowledged my existence before when I had been consciously trying to curry favour. Now that I might be opposed to him, he was all smiles.

"I'm so sorry we couldn't take you on here," he said.

"Not to worry."

"You don't need me to tell you that you were excellent."

"That's very kind of you," I said.

He was quite right – he hadn't felt the need to say anything to me in the months we had worked in the same building, let alone mention that I was any good.

"It's just that, you know... "

"Yes."

"And Silas is very good indeed."

"He certainly is. I keep telling him exactly that. But he's too polite to accept it."

"Anyway. What about you? I don't imagine you've had much difficulty getting tenancy somewhere else."

"Well, I have actually. I tried a few and they weren't very keen on me."

"If you keep on trying, I'm sure it'll be all right in the end."

"I'm not sure it will be. But anyway I'm not trying anymore."

"What?"

"I might try and do some libel reading at a newspaper or perhaps try to become a journalist."

"Oh. Well, I can't pretend I have any sway in that world. But I could certainly recommend you to other chambers."

"That's very kind of you, but really don't bother."

"You've really given up on the whole idea of being a barrister?"

"Yes."

"Still, having rights of audience is a useful thing. Being a member of an Inn, even if you never practise, can also be useful. Access to the libraries, the dining halls, contacts... And, you know, even if you don't get in here, there's always a chance you might get in somewhere else, particularly if you got a good reference from a previous chambers."

His words were unusually polite and friendly, but behind them there was a seam of ill-will. It was a form of plea bargaining: don't take out an action and I'll help you; take one and I'll confiscate your rights of audience – the certificate that gave you the ability to appear in court – and membership of the Inn.

"Well, I suppose I might consider an action," I said. "But I'll wait until the minimum-payment case goes to appeal."

"If you do sue, we probably won't have much of a defence." He paused and took a swift breath. "But we will use everything in our power to defend the action and we will dispute anything that's in doubt, like your time sheet."

He pointed to the piece of paper he had asked me to bring in, with the details of the hours I had worked.

"Oh, and by the way," he added, laughing at my legal knowledge. "It's unlikely to go to appeal. The girl's chambers is supporting the action."

He was right, I found out when I went and looked the case up in the *Times*. Occasionally a friendly defendant will side with the plaintiff, purely in the interests of getting a judge to decide on a new point of law. Friendly actions don't actually mean opposing barristers are actually friendly to each other. They are still getting paid, and so a friendly action is likely to go on just as long as an unfriendly one.

As Dickens wrote in the foreword to *Bleak House*, where he was trying to justify the ludicrous-sounding extremes of *Jarndyce v Jarndyce*:

> At the present moment there is a suit before the Court which was commenced nearly 20 years ago; in which from 30 to 40 counsel have been known to appear at one time; in which costs have been incurred to the amount of £70,000; which is a friendly suit; and which is (I am assured) no nearer to its termination now than when it was begun. There is another well-known suit in Chancery, not yet decided, which was commenced before the close of the last century, and in which more than double

the amount of £70,000 has been swallowed up in costs. If I wanted other authorities for *Jarndyce v Jarndyce*, I could rain them on these pages, to the shame of – a parsimonious public.

However shameful, lavish and positively unfriendly friendly suits got, Garton was right. The fact that the minimum-payment case was a friendly one meant I was almost certain to win if I did take out an action.

As a result, I went as far as looking up the pupil's case in the library – which carried fuller reports than the *Times* – and writing down the name of her solicitor, the one I should ring if I wanted to get a case going.

"I might be taking chambers to court," I told Sara over the phone.

"Don't," she said.

"Why not?"

"Have you listened to anything I've told you over the last year?" Sara said, adopting the *Playschool* voice again. "Don't... ever...go... to...court... It... is... madness!"

"But this is a friendly action."

"Repeat after me. "Don't... ever... go... to... court... It... is... madness!""

A mixture of laziness, procrastination and Sara's advice against ever going to law meant I delayed ringing the solicitor for months. Before I got round to it, Francis Garton rang up.

"You've heard about the case?"

"No."

"You were quite right," Garton said, a note of warmth in his voice. "She lost her appeal."

"Oh. Thanks very much for telling me."

"Not at all. That does mean you won't be taking out a case yourself?"

"I'm not sure I was ever going to."

"Not what you said before. Anyway, there really wouldn't be much point in you taking it on. Unlikely to go to the Lords."

"Thanks anyway."

"A pleasure," he said. I could hear his smile – which was unusual; I had never seen him smile in the six months we had spent having tea with each other every day. "And by the way, your time sheets were fine."

"That's good to hear."

And it was good to hear. Sad as I was that the pupil's brave stand against her own chambers hadn't succeeded, I was even crosser at the thought of that rare smile on Garton's face. Still, I had saved myself several thousand pounds in legal fees and I liked ro imagine Garton passing long evenings working out how many hours I had spent in his chambers over the last six months. Did I get in on the dot of nine on Friday morning at the height of the Christmas season when I might have been at a party the night before? Did I really stay until six every day in August, even when my pupilmaster, and the whole of chambers, were in Cornwall or Umbria?

It was also heartening to have got the law right, to have predicted that the case would go to appeal, despite what Garton had said. I could see for a moment the satisfaction in working out the way a case, however open-and-shut it looks at the beginning, could tumble the other way in the end, once it has been put through the great mangle of the legal system. The pleasure was not great enough to make me think I had done the wrong thing in giving up. But it didn't make it any easier to make the break and know what to do next.

On the last weekend of my pupillage, at the end of September, I went alone to a cottage in south-west Wales near Pembroke that belonged to my parents. Not sure what to do with the future but not wanting to discuss it with anyone, I got into a bit of a state, going over my options again and again. They were pretty straightforward:

1. Continue trying to get a pupillage? No – how could I wilfully undergo another half-century full of years like the one I had just had?

2. Do something else? Yes, but...

3. ...what?

For three days, I bicycled the lanes of Pembrokeshire, thinking about these three questions constantly; or, more accurately, just asking myself them constantly. I never developed the consequences of each scenario or looked at each one in detail; I just asked, asked, asked, and despaired, despaired, despaired.

On the third day, stretching out the time before I had to head back to London and an empty future, I took one last bike ride at about seven in the evening. Freewheeling down a little dip in a ridge overlooking the Bristol Channel, I passed an open gate. Out of the corner of my eye, I caught a glimpse of a flurry of activity: unusual here, where the fields were as empty as the roads. Doubling back, I went and had a look. There was a great flock of swallows – twenty or thirty strong – darting back and forth over the field, swooping in arrow-straight lines along the hedgerows, whirling past my face at the corner of the field where I stood. I stared at them for ten minutes, transfixed as their circuits dropped lower and lower, in line with their insect prey who flew 50 foot above the ground at midday and dropped below my knees as the night drew in.

Mesmerised as I was by the birds, my mind could never be completely engaged by them because it was already engaged by something else: the three questions. They had become so all-consuming that everything else – my dealings with sex, food, friends, family... everything – was changed by what was going on at work.

Should I meet my oldest schoolfriend for lunch? No, I couldn't possibly. He'd be bound to bring up question number three as soon as we sat down.

Should I call up the pretty girl who was, an ally told me, keen on the idea of being called up? Don't be stupid. What sort of girl is interested in the sort of unemployed man who might not be able to buy her dinner?

Even my view of the swallows was stained by the three questions. Here was heart-stopping beauty, with nature dutifully doing all that it's supposed to do; the whole, well-oiled food chain turning smoothly, with the swallows nicely fattening up on bugs just before they made their 3,000-mile trip south to Africa for the winter. Everything in its proper place, and a proper place for everything. Except for me, me, me, and questions one, two and three.

Envious as I was of the lucky swallows – I loved staring at them – I don't think I could ever have had my fill. Looking at them, while nagging myself to bicycle away and do the right thing – get back to London and face my uncertain future before it got too ridiculously late to do the four-

and-a-half-hour journey – was like eating a pack of crisps and wanting another, knowing they were bad for you.

After a small inner battle, I suddenly turned to go, with a burst of willpower, like the one that strikes you when you decide manfully not to have another crisp. As I picked up my bike, I caught sight of a brown paper bag that had been lying by my right foot for the whole time I had been standing there. The bag was sodden with evening dew, but inside all was pristine – a mint, unopened copy of *Fat and Fifty*, a porn mag devoted to women with both these characteristics.

Laughter is a social function for humans. You very rarely do it on your own; possibly at a book or at the telly, but even then it's likely to be an internal harrumphy laugh. But I laughed out loud at finding the copy of *Fat and Fifty*. The laugh didn't last long but it was intense. The effect on my mind was intense, too, intense enough for the first time in a year to drown out the horrors, first of doing a job I hated, and now of dealing with the life that awaited me at the end of the M4.

For a second or two, the discovery of *Fat and*

Fifty blanked out all the other great mish-mash of competing thoughts swilling around my head: my joy at the skill and beauty of the swallows, now practically hugging the ground, mixed with envy of their certainty and their winter holiday in Kenya.

What had happened to the poor owner of *Fat and Fifty*? I imagined him to be a middle-aged man, perhaps fat and 50 himself, who'd gone on a shopping trip to Pembroke with his elderly mother. While she bought the fruit and veg at Wisebuys, he nipped into Dave & Helen's, the newsagent's across the road, to get her *Western Telegraph* and his magazine in its discreet wrapper, and put them in his bag. And then, driving back together to the family farm, him at the wheel, mother in the passenger seat, she asked him to pass the bag with her *Telegraph* in it. In a deft movement, belying his age (50) and his size (fat), as the car dropped into the dip in the ridge that overlooked the Bristol Channel, he must have slipped the brown paper bag out of the shopping bag, hurled it through a gap in the hedge, and passed the Dave & Helen's bag to his mother.

"What was that, dear?" she might have said.

"Oh, must have been a swallow. Lot of them about at this time of year."

***

Driving back to London that night, I phoned Silas at 10pm from Leigh Delamere service station, to wish him luck for the next day, his first as a tenant.

I told him about the swallows and he showed polite interest. I moved on to *Fat and Fifty* and my mother-and-son scenario.

"Absolutely classic. Better than clouds and silver linings."

"What?"

"It's always annoyed me. Clouds and their silver linings are two separate things. And so people just use the expression to say, first a bad thing's going to happen, and then a good thing's going to happen."

"Well, thanks very much. That's not much consolation for the bad thing."

"The *Fat and Fifty* moment is much better: something absolutely terrible happens and, at exactly the same moment, something fantastically funny happens. The Welsh farmer couldn't have been more horrified. And you couldn't have been more delighted.

"And it could have been even more wonderful: imagine if, say, for example, you were interested in porn."

"Just imagine. Ludicrous."

"Absolutely ridiculous."

We moved on to talk briefly about his new tenancy and, even more briefly, about question number three – what was I going to do?

"I've thought about nothing else for three days," I said, "and I still haven't got an answer."

"For a year, actually."

"No. You know I tried desperately hard to like it for a long time."

"Yup. But as soon as you realised you hated it, you must have been thinking of other things."

"No. I tried to put it off. Even now, I'm still putting it off."

"Well, you'll have to think about it soon."

"Silas!"

"What?"

"It's not like you to be so aggressive."

"I'm not. It's good that you'll be forced to think about it; because you'll end up doing something you like."

"It's not good. It's terrifying."

"It's terrifying and good – a real *Fat and Fifty* moment."

***

Silas was right. My difficulties turned out to be prime *Fat and Fifty* material.

Unable to face doing what I'd hated – staying at the Bar – and unwilling to do nothing, I stumbled my way into doing something I liked. Over the course of the year, I had occasionally been given book reviews to do by the *Times Literary Supplement*, where I had worked for a few months eight years before.

As a new boy, I got given unknown novels to review and was asked to write only a few hundred words about them for the "In Brief" pages – a double-page spread with about five reviews on each page. I spent all the hours I could, trying to write well and accurately and entertainingly about these books. I might spend 20 or 30 hours, reading and writing about one novel. A good barrister would have been paid about £5,000 for that amount of work; a junior one about £1,000. The going rate for an "In Brief" review at the *TLS* was £25. It seemed fantastically generous – I would have done it for nothing.

The closest I could get to carving out a job that had something to do with writing was on a gossip column, in this case on the "Peterborough" column, now "London Spy", in the *Daily Telegraph*. I had my first day there in May, seven months of loafing and uncertainty after I left the Bar. An hour after turning up at the *Telegraph*'s Canary Wharf offices, the direct and appealing Scottish secretary on "Peterborough" waved a white card in the air.

"Launch of Kingsley Amis's *Letters*. Tonight at the Garrick, anyone?"

"I'd love to go. If no one else wants to."

"No. It's yours. Should be excellent. Lots of good names."

And it was. Kingsley Amis was, after Evelyn Waugh, my favourite writer, and there I was, talking to his friends, drinking Chablis, and being paid for it.

After a few minutes of circling Martin Amis, another favourite novelist, and trying to think up a clever and original enough question, I pounced.

"I'm sorry to bother you. I'm Harry Mount from

'Peterborough'," I said quickly, jumping into my clever question before he could tell me to go away. "I was wondering what effect Philip Larkin's death had on your father." Martin Amis paused, and then said in deep, perfectly modulated words, as if he was dictating a passage from his memoirs: "My father depended on a holy triumvirate of crutches: the drinks cabinet, the television and Philip. When one of the crutches went, I think he was destabilised."

***

Most mothers, if asked whether they would like their sons to be barristers or gossip columnists, would not need much time to think. But there, at the Garrick, on an unseasonably warm evening – I sweated heavily while talking to Martin Amis, and not just out of nerves – I realised why I was different from most mothers. Talking to a writer I admired about the relationship between my favourite poet and my almost-favourite novelist had me on my mettle, and nervous, and excited, and thoughtful, and smug, and proud. I had been nervous plenty of times as a pupil barrister, but never any of the other adjectives. I had done what I thought was impossible – I HAD FOUND SOMETHING I LIKED DOING!

EPILOGUE

I suffer from extreme bouts of grass-is-greener-itis. When I resolved not to keep on trying to get a legal job, I knew I had done the right thing. But still, given this strange medical complaint, there was a strong chance that I would look back some time in the future and think that I had given up something wonderful.

So I preserved my thoughts of how I looked back at my year as a pupil at the moment when it had ended, before I had become a journalist, to make sure I didn't start to mythologise my time as a lawyer. I copied the style of Evelyn Waugh, who had a good way of looking back at the passing of a year. On October 28th 1942, his 39th birthday, he wrote in his diary:

A good year. I have begotten a fine daughter, published a successful book, drunk 300 bottles of wine and smoked 300 or more Havana cigars. I have got back to soldiering among friends. I have about £900 in hand and no grave debts except to the Government; health excellent except when impaired by wine; a wife I love, agreeable work in surroundings of great beauty. Well, that is as much as one can hope for.

In imitation, I wrote the following passage in my diary for October 1st – the day after I talked to Silas about my *Fat and Fifty* moment. It was the last time I ever spoke to him. Until 9am that morning, we were both strictly still pupils and so were on a sort of level. After 9am, he was a tenant; after 9am, I remained a barrister – as you do for life – but I would never be a practising one. Despite our shared flippancy about the whole enterprise; despite his self-deprecation about the job and my lack of desire to do it; despite all this, the fact that he had remained in the job I hated – and he had prospered while I had failed – meant we were split for good.

October 1st

A bad year. I have begotten nothing and produced nothing. I have chucked in a legal career – I was really an office boy – and I have nothing but loafing lined up ahead of me; although I can afford to do it with my savings, I am too afraid of being considered a wastrel to do some interesting bits of loafing, and go abroad or do anything pleasurable.

The best moments in the last year have been drunken ones (especially at parties) of which there have probably been about 60 good examples. I am earning no money, except for the odd book review. I have put on about half a stone and the process doesn't look like stopping.

No girlfriend.

But do not in the future, as you sit alone in a moment of despair, get worried at the thought you might be considered a loser. You will never again be forced to read these words: "Reasonable financial provision – s.1(2)(b) such financial provision as it would be reasonable in all the circumstances of the case of the applicant to receive for his maintenance."

I'M A TEACHER
GET ME OUT OF HERE!
Francis Gilbert

At last, here it is. The book that tells you the unvarnished truth
about teaching. By turns hilarious, sobering, and downright
horrifying, I'm a Teacher, Get me Out of Here! contains the
sort of information that you won't find in any school
prospectus, government advert or Hollywood film.

Francis Gilbert candidly describes the remarkable way in
which he was trained to be a teacher, his terrifying first lesson
and his even more frightening experiences in his first job at
Truss comprehensive, one of the worst schools in the country.
Follow him on his rollercoaster journey through the world that
is the English education system; encounter thuggish and
charming children, terrible and brilliant teachers; learn about
the sinister effects of school inspectors and the teacher's disease
of 'controloholism'. Spy on what really goes on behind the
closed doors of inner-city schools.

"A fascinating and finely observed account of
an inner city school."
Peter Ackroyd

1-904095-68-2

GOING BUDDHIST
Panic and emptiness, the Buddha and me
Peter J Conradi

About twenty years ago, Peter Conradi's life hit the bumpers, and he began suffering from terrifying panic attacks. This book is his account of the new life-journey he embarked on back then, when, with the help of his friend and mentor Iris Murdoch, he began to explore Buddhism.

Each year in the UK, as Conradi describes, 22 million prescriptions are written for tranquillisers, and yet Buddhism can provide a third way. During meditation one's heart rate slows down and brain rhythms become calmer.

Full of wise comedy, this is a self-help book for cynics, in which Conradi seeks to explain the beauty of Buddhism, a religion now more relevant than ever to Westerners, perishing from the nihilism of the age.

"...a short, sweet and enchanting book... Conradi's account of his epiphany is an inspiration."
Mick Brown, DAILY TELEGRAPH

1-904095-63-1